What People Are Saying...

Everyone should read this captivating story of Richard Sigmund's journey through the remarkable eternal home God has prepared for us. It is so detailed that you feel like you are right there with him. *My Time in Heaven* will enlighten your life and open your understanding to the glorious things of the living God. I highly recommend this book!

—Dr. Mary K. Baxter
Author, *A Divine Revelation of Hell*
and *A Divine Revelation of Heaven*

For over thirty years, I have interviewed people who have visited heaven. Richard Sigmund has the most thorough and detailed description I have ever heard. He answers the most mysteries about heaven of anyone I have ever interviewed. While Richard Sigmund was in heaven, he was told about my ministry and my future and that he would meet me. Two years ago, we became good friends! The prophetic time clock is one second before midnight, and this book will help us to be more heavenly-minded. A must-read!

—Sid Roth
Host, *It's Supernatural!* television program

I have been collecting books on heaven for over twenty-five years. I was excited and anticipating my first meeting with Richard Sigmund. We met and I was touched by his ministry. As we talked about his heaven experience, I could feel the anointing on the testimony of his time there. This book is easy to read and understand. Children love it. Adults recognize the anointing on it as they read. I have a friend who bought several hundred copies and gave them to the people who attended the funeral of his best friend's mother. What a comfort! I highly recommend this book. It is biblical and informative. Serving Jesus is the ultimate in life. Heaven is REAL!

—Paul Hegstrom, Ph.D.
Founder, Life Skills International
Author, *Angry Men and the Women Who Love Them*
and *Broken Children, Grown-Up Pain*

When Richard Sigmund was killed in a bad car wreck, he was dead eight hours. God took him to heaven. He sat at the Throne of God. He talked to Jesus. He saw the apostles and talked with them. He has the most extensive description of heaven of all. Richard makes God as close as the air you breathe! Having ministered throughout the world with him many times, I know that his love for others causes him to pray for the sick until the last person has been touched by God. Heaven comes down, and God is glorified.

—Dr. Loretta Blasingame
Founder, Loretta Blasingame Ministries
Author, *Is Anybody Up There?*

Prepare yourself to see, through the words of his book, a panoramic view of the afterlife; and, at the same time, see intimate details of what life is like for the Christian when one steps over the threshold of death into the world beyond the veil of this planet. There is another world that is beautiful to behold, fascinating to the human mind, and indescribably peaceful. It is a land "beyond the sunset," where Jesus has made preparation for us to live eternally in the abundance of

His love and His grace. After you have read this book from beginning to end, read it again and again. Keep it as a valuable resource in your personal library. Acquire extra copies for your family and your friends. Always have *My Time in Heaven* close at hand. We are told that one of the basic fears of many people is the fear of death. *My Time in Heaven* is a special book, with a special message, revealed under special circumstances to a man called by God to be a modern-day prophet. I love the message of *My Time in Heaven*.

—Dr. Paul C. Collins, M.Div., Th.D.
Founder, Acts Ministry

Dr. Richard Sigmund has one of the most miraculous ministries I've ever seen. So miraculous, in fact, that some of the miracles have truly staggered the imagination and challenged the faith of many because they were so astounding. The testimony of his death experience and going to heaven is the best I have ever heard. I know that Dr. Sigmund's primary concern is to help the suffering to receive healing from the living Christ.

—L. D. Kramer, D.D., D.Min.
Pioneer television evangelist
Senior Pastor, Rejoice Christian Center,
Burnsville, Minnesota

This book has a powerful anointing on it! I felt like I was walking through heaven and experiencing it myself. It makes my soul yearn to behold this beautiful home Jesus has prepared for me.

—B. G.

This book has completely changed my life. We all have questions about what heaven will be like. And to have a first-hand, eyewitness account is incredibly powerful. I feel as though I am on fire with the need to spread the Word of God to everyone I know. I have been afraid of offending people by speaking to them about Jesus Christ. I know and love Jesus and recognize all the miracles and works happening in my life. I share these with the people I know when the opportunity arises. But now I feel the need to share with them what I've read in your book. I say to them, "I've just finished reading the most incredible book." Then, the conversations begin! Praise God! Thank you for writing such a wonderful book. And thank God and His Son Jesus Christ for taking you to heaven, showing you around, and allowing you to come back and share it with the rest of us!

—C.

I cannot put into words the impact this book has had on my family, friends, and coworkers. God speaks loud and clear through it! I just want you to know how mightily God is using your faithfulness to do as He has asked.

—C. C.

Your book is a great blessing! I look forward to my new home in heaven someday. A book like this really makes heaven and the Lord more of a reality.

—N. S.

I had lost hope in everything in this world, but after I reading this book, it renewed my faith in the Lord. And whenever things are not going the way I want, I remember there is "a place called heaven"!

—P. A.

Your book has touched my heart and reinforced my faith in the Lord. You have given me a gift, and I will cherish it forever.

—T. K.

Thank you for putting into a book your experience in heaven. In the last four months, I have had four family members enter through the veil that you wrote about. I shared this book with my family and friends. It is a source of comfort to both the believer in the Lord Jesus Christ and also the nonbeliever. To believers, it is confirmation as to where their departed loved ones are and also where they will one day be. To nonbelievers, it provides the knowledge that they, too, can gain entrance into God's heaven by receiving the Lord Jesus into their own hearts.

—R. C.

Thanks to the Lord that He was able to bring you back to life to share His wonderful and magnificent glory up in heaven. It's a book everyone should read.

—C. R.

I am an ex-everything. God found me in a Texas prison. I was skeptical at first. Brother Sigmund, I am writing to confess that your book has left an indelible imprint on my heart. I could not put it down. I'm grateful, and yet envious, that God allowed you to not only see, but also tour the other side. I love Jesus and do look forward to spending eternity with Him and the whole heavenly crew.

—R. F.

While reading your book, I was inspired to seek God for His will for my life. I want to go to heaven when my time comes. I have lost all fear of death. I look forward to being with Jesus and seeing God's Throne. Your descriptions of heaven were very detailed. I am greatly impressed with this book. I have recommended it to my congregation. May God continue to inspire you to finish your ministry here on earth.

—Pastor William Smith
Stratford, Avon shire, England

MY TIME IN

HEAVEN

A TRUE STORY OF DYING...

AND COMING BACK

Richard SIGMUND

WHITAKER
HOUSE

MY TIME IN HEAVEN:
A True Story of Dying and Coming Back

ISBN: 978-1-60374-123-1
eBook ISBN: 978-1-60374-350-1
Printed in the United States of America
© 2004, 2010 by Cleft of the Rock Ministries

Whitaker House
1030 Hunt Valley Circle
New Kensington, PA 15068
www.whitakerhouse.com

Library of Congress Cataloging-in-Publication Data
Sigmund, Richard, 1941–2010
    My time in heaven / by Richard Sigmund.
        p. cm.
    Includes index.
    ISBN 978-1-60374-123-1 (trade pbk. : alk. paper) 1. Heaven—Christianity.
2. Future life—Christianity 3. Near-death experiences—Religious aspects—
Christianity. 4. Death—Religious aspects—Christianity. 5. Sigmund, Richard,
1941– I. Title.
    BT846.3.S54 2010
    236'.1092—dc22
    [B]
                                        2009042582

12 13 14 15 16 17 18 19 20 **ய** 29 28 27 26 25 24 23 22

Dedication

This book is dedicated to the many people who have encouraged and supported this project:

Norvel and Maggie Hayes

Sid Roth

Dr. L. D. Kramer, Challenge Ministries

Dr. Robert Cesarek, Love of God Ministries

And the special words of encouragement from:

Rex Humbard

W. V. Grant Sr.

David Nunn

Contents

Preface

I can't explain it. I can only tell you what I saw. And language fails. It really is indescribable: the sights, the sounds, the sizes, the colors, the smells. How can one describe a place called heaven?

I remember knowing things there that I can't remember now—or am not supposed to remember. I was allowed to see many things, but there was much more that I was not allowed to see.

Many others have had similar experiences of heaven, and some of the things they saw were the same as what I saw. Others were not. And if you were shown a place called heaven, you would see different things, too. Everybody who has an experience like this is going to see it differently. Many of the things that I saw and witnessed would probably not be the things that another person would see because we are each individuals, and God deals with us in individual ways.

The things that I saw related and ministered to me, and I believe they will also minister to those who read this book. Jesus told me, "Don't ever forget how much I love you and what I have done for you. Never forget how much I love those whom you are going back to and the place I have prepared for them and how much I love them."

I can't explain it. I can only tell you what I saw. And I can tell only so much.

—Rev. Richard Sigmund

Introduction
"Suddenly, I Was in a Thick, Cloudy Veil"

There was a sheet over my face.

Oh, did I hurt!

"He's been dead all these hours," I heard.

I sat up and said, "I ain't dead yet."

A medical attendant screamed. Another lost bladder control. Apparently, I had been dead for over eight hours, and they were wheeling me down to the morgue.

I could feel my bones knitting together. I could feel the scars healing while I sat up. And I breathed and spoke.

*****

It was October 17, 1974, and I was driving back to the church in Bartlesville, Oklahoma, where I was ministering. At this time in my life, God was speaking to me about the concept of blind, instant obedience—being broken before Him, as a wild horse is broken. I'd been having an argument with God about being obedient. God had told me to give a word of warning to someone, and I didn't want to do it. I drove to see the person, but I kept avoiding contact with him and left without ever telling him. There were also several other issues in my life. I was having trouble with my wife back in Arizona—big trouble.

The vehicle I was driving was a rather plush luxury van. It was large, the kind that featured one of those 1970s custom-built TVs that hung down by an arm from the ceiling.

Suddenly, without warning, I was in a thick, cloudy veil. I didn't realize it at the time, but I had been in a deadly, one-car accident.

1

"You Have an Appointment with God"

"You have come to Mount Zion, to the heavenly Jerusalem, the city of the living God. You have come to thousands upon thousands of angels in joyful assembly, to the church of the firstborn, whose names are written in heaven. You have come to God, the judge of all men, to the spirits of righteous men made perfect, to Jesus the mediator of a new covenant, and to the sprinkled blood that speaks a better word than the blood of Abel."

—Hebrews 12:22–24

I had been driving down the road in my van, but all of a sudden, I was in a veil. It was like a thick cloud. There were gold, purple, and amber colors and a bright light. The cloud pulsated as sound was going through it. And I was going through it, too.

Behind me, I could hear people talking. They were only a few inches away. There were sirens. Lots of noise. And I heard the words, "He's dead."

DRAWN THROUGH A GLORY CLOUD

A force was drawing me through a glory cloud, and on the other side of the cloud I could hear people singing. There was laughter with great joy, and I was in total peace.

I smelled an aroma—and experienced a taste—like strawberries and cream.

For what seemed like a few minutes, I was moving through the cloud, and yet the cloud was moving through me. Then, I turned to my right to what appeared to be a receiving area.

HEAVEN'S RECEIVING AREA

Reunion of Family Members

Just a few feet from me, I could see two women standing. Somehow, I knew that they were of great age, but their countenances were like they were in their mid-twenties, and they were beautiful. They were hugging each other and seemed very joyful, and they were looking through the veil.

"He is coming; I see him. He is coming. Here he comes."

In heaven, I was in total peace.

Suddenly, a man came through the veil. He had a look of profound confusion for a moment. He didn't know where he was. But, just as suddenly, he looked at the women and recognized them. They began to hug him and to praise and worship God. You could tell it was a joyous reunion.

Reunion of a Pastor and Church Members

Further to the right, I noticed a group of about fifty people. They, too, were worshipping God. Many were standing there with their arms up just praising Him. Some were hugging each other and saying, "Here he comes; I see him coming."

They were apparently waiting for their pastor, who had just died. Suddenly, he was in the veil. When he first appeared, he looked like a very old man. But, as suddenly as he appeared into the heavenly atmosphere, all of the age lines in his face disappeared, and his gnarled little body straightened up. This very old pastor now looked as if he was in his mid- to late twenties; his youth had been renewed. He just stood there, bewildered. But, in a moment, it dawned on him that he was in heaven, and he began to rejoice. He said, "I want to see Jesus. Where is my Jesus? I want to see the Lord." People began to hug him and rejoice with him.

"Oh, it is you, brother, and it is you, sister," he said as he called them by name. And he said again, "I want to see Jesus."

Someone told him, "Oh, He is just a little further down your pathway. You will meet with Him. He is always there, right on time."

Reunion of Mother and Baby

My attention was drawn to a group of about thirty-five people. They were standing in front of the veil, waiting for someone special to appear. I could tell that everyone was in an excited and joyous spirit.

There were those gathered who evidently had died many earth years ago, but here, it was only yesterday. I saw people who must have been this special person's children, sister, and husband, who had long since become residents of heaven.

"There she is," someone said. A person in the group was carrying a baby. The baby had the full power of speech and was totally aware of all its surroundings. This baby cried with a high little voice, "Mommy! Mommy! There is my mommy. Jesus said that I could remain a baby and that Mommy could raise me in heaven."

How great is the love of God.

At that moment, an old, wrinkled woman, all stoop-shouldered and very frail, came through the veil. Instantly upon entering the atmosphere of heaven, she snapped completely straight—her frail, stooped-over body became just as straight as could be. Suddenly, she was once again a beautiful young woman, dressed in her radiant, pure white robe of glory.

Everyone cheered with shouts of joy as the little baby flew into her arms. They had been parted at childbirth. The woman had survived a concentration camp, but her baby had not.

Yet God, in His infinite mercy, saw to it that nothing was lost. The love of God is so great that no person could know it all. It truly is beyond finding out, and only eternity will tell it all. There were tears running down my cheeks, even though I was just an onlooker. I shared their joy, and I still do.

In His infinite mercy, God sees to it that nothing is lost.

Greeted in Heaven by People and Angels

As I understand it, no one has ever come to heaven without having other people greet him or her (except, of course, for Abel, the first person to die and enter heaven).

Then, I noticed that there were not only people greeting the pastor who had just come through the veil, but also angels. And there were angels for the others who came through. All up and down the veil, people were coming through. And there were always angels to meet them.

Evidently, you can see through the veil from heaven, but you can't see through it from earth. In other words, from our existence, you can't see through the veil. In heaven, you know when someone is coming through. People in heaven somehow knew that they should be at the receiving area when someone was coming. Later, I learned that there are announcement centers in heaven, and people are notified that their loved ones are about to arrive there. I will explain more about these announcement centers in another chapter.

A PATH PREPARED FOR ME

The veil extended as far to the left and right as I could see. I had the impression that it was hundreds of miles long in each direction. And every few feet, there was a path leading into heaven. Everyone who came through the veil had a path unique for him or her. And I had a path—the path was for me.

Then, from behind me, I heard a voice saying, "You have an appointment with God," and I felt a familiar touch.

Although I could not see who was behind me, I believe it was the Lord Jesus. I recognized His voice.

— 2 —
"You Must Walk on This Path"

*"He guides me in paths of righteousness
for his name's sake."*

—Psalm 23:3

Imust be in a place called heaven! I thought. *What a wonderful, wonderful place.*

I was standing on a golden pathway.

"You must walk on this path." The voice, gentle yet firm, made it clear that I needed to be on this path. I wasn't about to argue with the voice, which, again, seemed to me to be the voice of Jesus.

On the pathway, I was always accompanied by at least two angels: one on the right and one on the left. My impression was that the angel on the right was there mostly to explain things. The one on the left didn't say much except for reminding me frequently that I had an appointment with God. I believe that he was my guardian angel. We all have guardian angels who are assigned to us at birth. These two angels had separate jobs, but they worked in perfect harmony.

The Golden Pathway and Garden

The golden pathway was like a guided tour. It led me in a particular direction in which I had to go. It would take me to things that I was supposed to see before my appointment with God.

The pathway was about six feet wide, and there was dimension to it—thickness. I was walking through a garden that stretched for as far as I could see in either direction. And I saw great groups of people.

> **There is no death in heaven. God Himself is our life.**

On either side of the pathway was the richest turf-green grass I had ever seen. And it was moving with life and energy. Supernaturally, I knew that if I picked a blade of grass and then put it back down, it would just keep on growing.

There is no death in heaven. Not even for a blade of grass. Death is impossible there because heaven is a place of eternal life. Heaven is a place where the life of God sustains everything; God Himself is our life, and He is eternal. He has no beginning, and He can have no end.

For the wages of sin is death, but the gift of God is eternal life in Christ Jesus our Lord.   (Romans 6:23)

For in him [God] *we live and move and have our being.*   (Acts 17:28)

There were flowers of every imaginable size and color along the path. There were banks and banks of flowers. Some were the size of a dinner table! There were roses that looked about four feet across and might have weighed fifty pounds on earth. And as I walked, the flowers faced me. The air was filled with their aroma, and they were all humming. I asked if I could pick one to smell, and I was told that I could. It was wonderful. When I put the flower down, it was immediately replanted and growing again. Again, there is no death in heaven.

As I walked along the golden pathway, I noticed the sky. It was rosette-pinkish in color, but it was also a crystal clear blue. And there were clouds in the sky—clouds of glory. When I looked more closely at them, I saw that the "clouds" were actually thousands of angels and thousands upon thousands of people walking in groups and singing. They were strolling in the sky.

There was a park, which had benches where you could sit and talk to others. These benches were everywhere. They were made of some type of solid gold, but their shape reminded me of wrought-iron lawn furniture. People were sitting and talking and praising God. They were having a wonderful time talking with people who had just come through the veil. Others were there in great groups waiting for their loved ones to come through.

All the people there were in preparation of loved ones coming into heaven. I heard someone say, "When he sees his mansion, he is going to shout glory."

Something just went all through me, and I thought, *Maybe God has some place for me up here in heaven.*

THE TREES OF HEAVEN

The beautifully manicured park was filled with huge, striking trees. They had to be at least two thousand feet tall. And there were many different varieties. Some I knew; others, I had no idea what species they were. But they were tall and strong, with no dead branches or limbs. There was not even a dead leaf. Some of the leaves on the trees were shaped like huge diamonds.

One tree that caught my attention was crystal clear and huge—it seemed to be miles and miles across. I was told that it was a Diadem tree. Each leaf on this tree was the shape of a teardrop, like a crystal chandelier. And there was a continual sound of chimes coming from the leaves as they brushed against one another in the gentle breeze—the beautiful sound of crystal. When I touched them, there was a glow as the sound emanated from them.

But there was more. Each leaf, each limb—the entire tree—gave off a tremendous glow with all the colors that were in the glory cloud. The tree glowed with sound and light. It was also aflame with glory. The flame started in the root and went all the way through the branches and out into the chandelier-like leaves. The tree exploded in a cloud of glory—a beautiful light. And it exploded with sound—an unbelievably beautiful sound.

The Diadem tree was glorious. Under it were what looked like tens of thousands of people worshipping. They were not worshipping the tree, but only God.

The further I went toward the Throne of God, which the path was leading me to, the more trees I saw. Each was as glorious as the Diadem tree.

I went up to what I thought was a walnut tree, and I was told to take and eat. The fruit was pear shaped and copper colored. When I picked it, another fruit instantly grew in its place.

When I touched the fruit to my lips, it evaporated and melted into the most delicious thing I had ever tasted. It was like honey, peach juice, and pear juice. It was sweet but not sugary. My face was filled with the juice from the fruit. But nothing, by any means, can defile a person in heaven. Immediately, the juice from the beautiful, sweet tree's fruit ran down my throat like honey. My face was just covered all over with this beautiful, wonderful liquid that the fruit had turned into. Whatever it was, in that atmosphere of heaven, it was also instantly gone. It was a wonderful experience, and I can almost still taste that delicious juice after all this time.

I was strengthened the moment I smelled the beautiful fragrance of the leaf.

There were also trees whose leaves were shaped like hearts and gave off a beautiful aroma. I was told to take a leaf and smell it, and so I did. Then, a voice told me that it would give me strength to carry on. The moment I smelled the beautiful fragrance, I was strengthened.

I had an overpowering urge to see Jesus. "Please, let me see Jesus," I said.

3

The Lamb's Book of Life

*"He who overcomes will, like them, be dressed
in white. I will never blot out his name from the
book of life, but will acknowledge his name
before my Father and his angels."*

—Revelation 3:5

The angel walking with me gestured and said, "Behold
the wall." The wall was tall, and it looked as if it was a
mile away.

Suddenly, I was at the wall. (Travel in heaven seems to be
at the speed of thought.)

"BEHOLD THE BOOKS"

Then, the angel said, "Behold the books."

On the left, a book was sitting on golden pillars that served
as a giant easel. The book had to be a mile high and three
quarters of a mile wide. It was huge. And angels turned the
pages of the book.

On the right was another book, which was the Lamb's
Book of Life. Its pages were turned, and I was lifted up to
see what was written on the open page. There, in three-inch
golden letters outlined in crimson red, was my name:

RICHARD OF THE FAMILY OF SIGMUND: SERVANT OF GOD

Alongside my name were the dates of my birth and my
conversion. The crimson-red outline on my name was the
sacrificed blood of Christ.

Nothing impure will ever enter it [the Holy City], *nor will anyone who does what is shameful or deceitful, but only those whose names are written in the Lamb's book of life.*   (Revelation 21:27)

I went up to the wall and saw that it was filled with all types of precious jewels: jasper, sardonyx, diamonds, yellowish gold emeralds, bloodstone diamonds. The wall was made of some type of stone material that gave off a sensation. When I touched the wall, it caressed my fingers.

GATES WITH TONGUES OF FIRE

I was then told to go to the gates.

The gates were huge; they seemed to be twenty-five miles high. And there were three tongues of fire on each gate, representing the Father, the Son, and the Holy Spirit. The gates were made of gold, which was fashioned similarly to wrought iron—curved on the top, with vertical stringers and filigree between the stringers at the bottom. The gold represented the great mercy of God. Thousands of individual pathways came to the gates.

FLOATING ON AIR AND IN CRYSTAL CLEAR WATER

Through the gate along my pathway were many beautiful houses—mansions. They had many verandas on the second, third, and even fourth floors. People would casually stroll off the edges of their verandas and effortlessly float to the ground. Or they would stay in the air. It seemed they could do either. The laws of physics don't seem to apply in heaven.

I was taken to a small lake, where I noticed that people were out in the water and even floating below its surface.

There were no waves on the lake, and the water was crystal clear and beautiful. It seemed even clearer than air is here.

The water was beautiful and even clearer than air is on earth.

The lake appeared to be bottomless, and it gave off a glow from the interior. I don't know what was down there, but it was glorious. Glory soil? Glowing rocks of jewels? Again, I don't know. But the water was alive.

I didn't go into the water, but I did dip my hand in it. The water had texture to it, and, like the wall of stone, it caressed my hand. It was refreshing—like putting your hand in chilled 7 Up, although it was at room temperature. A glorious experience.

People approached this water without fear. I saw what looked like millions of people down in the water walking, floating hand in hand, or even swimming. They could breathe under the crystal clear water. When they came out of the water, they were instantly dry.

Since there is no death in heaven, no one can die, even when underwater. Children can play in the water without fear of drowning. There are no dangerous water bugs or snakes. Nothing in heaven can harm you.

I later learned that at the Throne of God, there are four rivers. This lake is fed by one of the rivers, which is hundreds of yards wide and very deep in some places but shallow in others. As the river flows out from the Throne, the water begins to multiply.

JESUS SEEMED TO BE EVERYWHERE

The golden pathway led to buildings further ahead. Suddenly, I was there. The pathway stopped at a street made of a clear substance: it was like a jewel, intermingled with strands of gold. This road looked like a main street in a town. I was then taken to a group of people, and I noticed them watching my wonderment at the sights I saw.

Every now and then, as I traveled down the pathway, I would get a glimpse of Jesus just a little way ahead. He was talking with people, loving them, hugging them. They were looking at Him with such expressions of adoration and worship that I wanted to be there just to fall at His feet. Yet the angel would say, "Just a little further on down the path. You have an appointment with God, and you will meet with the Lord." The anticipation was bubbling up within me. I just wanted to be with Jesus. But I knew I had to wait.

In heaven, everybody has a turn to see Jesus directly, and, therefore, nobody is anxious about it. They are excited about the thought of seeing Him, but they are respectful of other people's turns to meet with Him; nobody tries to crowd ahead of anyone else. I felt great tranquility because

> *In heaven, everybody has a turn to see Jesus directly.*

I knew that when it was my turn, it would be a glorious moment for all eternity. I would join with the others who, in that moment of ecstasy, would get to see Jesus and talk with Him.

Yet this was the remarkable thing: though I could see Jesus ahead of me, I could not say that He was not also right behind me. He moved at what seemed to be the speed of light. There was only one of Him, but Jesus seemed to be everywhere at the same time. And I just wanted to be with Him.

—— 4 ——
Children and Babies in Heaven

*"Jesus said, 'Let the little children come to me,
and do not hinder them, for the kingdom of
heaven belongs to such as these.'"*

—Matthew 19:14

No child who dies is ever lost. Every one of them is with Jesus and enjoys His presence. Many times, I saw the Lord draw little children to Himself. He would hug them and talk with them. He seemed to be so refreshed that they were with Him.

A little girl who looked about eight years old and had beautiful, blonde hair came up to me. She knew me, and I recognized her, too: I remembered that she had died of cancer. I think she was some kind of ambassador in heaven because all she did was go from group to group and sing glorious songs.

"Brother Richard, do you want to see what I can do?" she asked. She proceeded to mess up her beautiful hair—hair that she had lost when she had suffered from cancer. When she stopped, it immediately returned to perfection. There are no "bad hair days" in heaven!

SPECIAL ABILITIES OF CHILDREN

Then, she said, "Brother Richard, would you like to hear me sing?"

She started singing in the most beautiful, powerful, soprano voice you could imagine. Heaven's ambassador was singing, and the choirs of heaven joined in. This was the most beautiful song I had ever heard—and the girl's talent was especially remarkable because of her apparently young age.

She was not the only child I saw. There were many others, each with abilities far greater than any adult's on earth. If you had been a good singer while you were on earth, then you could sing millions of times better in heaven. This little girl's ability exceeded that of anyone I had ever heard on earth.

In one place in heaven, I saw a young boy sitting before a piano that seemed to extend a hundred feet in every direction. It looked like a grand piano, yet in the middle of it stood an upright harp. Although he was not yet playing, this young boy was sitting there, and it was in an open place, like a courtyard, beside some homes. Then, he played the most beautiful music. It was a little like Bach, a little like Brahms, and a little like Beethoven. Yet I cannot tell you what the song was. When I left heaven, I left the tune there.

But there was music, and there were words to that song, and people joined in. While this child was playing the piano, the angels were standing at attention. Some had their arms raised, worshipping God. The notes of the song that this little boy was playing were reverberating throughout heaven. Choirs were joining in. It was unbelievable. It was glorious. And this little child was leading all of it.

I asked, "How can this be?"

One of the angels said to me, "They are playing this song because you are here. They want you to know that in heaven, even a child can learn things that are impossible to learn while on earth."

I was told, "Look at the little child."

As I looked at him, I noticed that he didn't appear to be older than seven or eight years of age. He turned to me, smiled, and waved his right hand while continuing to play with his left. Then, he stopped. The piano stopped, and the harp stopped. The people stopped. Everyone started to smile and praise the Lord. The song was over, but I could somehow hear it echoing. The boy said, "I can play anything I want to."

There was a beautiful children's choir in heaven. Again, the children had singing and musical capabilities far beyond anything you could imagine on earth. Every child could sing. I was told that the talents and abilities that God ordained for them from birth were, again, magnified millions of times over in heaven.

Our talents are magnified millions of times over in heaven.

At one point, I saw a child who looked about five years old sitting at an easel, painting a picture of the countryside. He would tell the paintbrush the color he wanted, and the paintbrush would turn to that color. The boy would say, for example, "No, darker. The tree must be darker." The paintbrush would turn to that color, and he would just wipe it across the canvas one time and the tree would appear. In heaven, all things are possible.

Raised in Heaven

Of the many children I saw in heaven, some looked like newborns—as if they had died during childbirth or shortly afterward, like the baby I had seen reunited with his mother when I first entered the veil. In heaven, these babies had the power of speech and were completely responsive. They knew and understood what you were saying to them and could reply. It was a most amazing thing to see.

The Nursery

I saw a number of children like this. They were being carried by angels or by other people. There was a nursery in heaven where I saw thousands, maybe millions, of children of that age. They were being tended to by angels and relatives and others. Remarkably, they grew up at a tremendous rate—they were not babies for very long.

Sometimes, I saw small groups of children; other times, I saw very large groups of them. All the children were very happy. Their hair and clothing were perfect. Some had little playsuits on, and some wore robes.

Playing Games

I saw children who were old enough to walk and run and play, and they played just as they would on earth. It seemed mandatory that the children play and have a good time—that they be *children*. They seemed to have the ability to be completely content just being children.

We know that on earth, if you don't experience a proper childhood, it is likely that you will struggle as an adult. You can be wounded in childhood and never fully mature emotionally in adulthood. But in heaven, since everything is perfect, children experience perfect childhoods. And they are welcome everywhere and around everyone—everybody loves the children, and the children love everybody.

In one of the games the children played, they would form a circle—sometimes with just a few children and other times with many children. A child would be selected, and he or she would float in the air, right in the middle of the circle. Another child would give the floater a little shove, and he or she would begin to float back and forth. All the children giggled with great glee. The child floating through the air would laugh and giggle. It seemed to be a wonderful experience for them. It would have been a great experience for me.

Another game was to see how far they could jump. Children would jump a hundred or two hundred feet in the air and float down like butterflies. It was an amazing sight.

I didn't see anyone play baseball, but I did see children climb tall trees and jump out of them, floating down like little cotton balls. It was great excitement for them. No harm could come to them—they were in no possible danger.

I saw children playing along the shores of the seas and lakes. There are many lakes in heaven, and, again, there was no danger; no harm could befall them. They played in the water, on the water, and under the water; they swam through the water or just sat at the bottom of the lake. They were having a wonderful time playing with the rocks and building sand castles on the beach. What a wonderful childhood. Oh, to have been raised in heaven!

I also saw the Lord Himself come and hug many children and tell them cute little stories. They loved Jesus, and He loved them so very much.

I could not tell by looking at the children if they had ever been sick on earth. I am sure some had been. Yet in heaven, they were 100 percent healthy, with rosy little cheeks—cherublike—and they could run and play.

In one place, I saw children having footraces. They ran faster than a horse on earth can run. It was amazing. In another place, I saw them riding horses. The horses loved it, and they loved the children. The horses had the power of thought and the power of speech. It was a wonderful experience.

I saw children playing what looked like hide-and-seek. One would run and hide and the other children would find him or her—and then start the game all over. It was such a beautiful sight.

Attending School

I saw that, as the children grew older, they began to attend school, just as they do on earth. But the schools were amazing. I was not permitted to know what they were taught. A child in heaven is far above the highest level of intelligence here. Children would learn things that geniuses on earth could not possibly know or understand. I was spellbound at the thought of it. I was speechless. You may have difficulty believing this; however, it is something that I pass on to you.

Children in heaven learn things that geniuses on earth could not possibly know or understand.

In the distance, I saw a group of children who had grown older in heaven. I do not know at what rate children grow there. I was told that it was none of my business.

They were taking what looked like a cloud of glory and telling it what to become. Jesus was there, also, and He said, "Do this," and blew on it. The cloud became an explosion of glory, and two beautiful birds that resembled parrots flew out of it. The birds were pure white. They were about six feet long and as tall as a man. Immediately, they began to sing a song of praise. It seemed as though all of heaven joined in and sang along with them. This is only one of the countless events I witnessed that are beyond my ability to explain adequately. You cannot fully believe it without the help of the Holy Spirit.

I was not allowed to talk with any of the children except for the girl who sang. At the time, there was a purpose. Now, I don't know what that purpose was.

FRIENDLY AND LOVING

All the children were very friendly and loving. They called each other by their first names and were called by their first names. They also called the angels by name (although I can't remember any of the names). In heaven, everybody knows everybody, and knows them by name. Heaven is a place you want to go, and one of its most beautiful features is the children.

5

Heavenly Dwellings

"In my Father's house are many mansions:
if it were not so, I would have told you.
I go to prepare a place for you."

—John 14:2 (KJV)

On my way to the Throne of God, I saw an avenue just off the street I was walking on. It was a huge avenue that branched off a little bit to the right and merged with another main street. This avenue seemed to be two hundred fifty feet wide and extended for miles and miles, but I could plainly see the other end of it. People were walking up and down the beautiful, golden and crystal streets, which appeared to be made of diamonds or maybe one big diamond of some kind. You could see through this diamond; it had layers of gold and silver, and there were precious stones everywhere.

MISSIONARIES' MANSIONS

On this avenue, there were mansions beyond compare. I was told that they were for missionaries. Everything they'd given, they'd given to the Lord. I believe that in heaven, God rewards everything that we can't receive here on earth.

In heaven, God gives rewards that we can't receive on earth.

I do not know the names of those who lived on that street because I was not allowed to explore it, but I know that some of them had been modern-day missionaries.

Some had just recently died, and there were large groups of people welcoming them at the veil. I saw one coming who was dressed in a beautiful robe. One of the first things he did was to grab his clothes and say, "Oh, how beautiful. I am not in rags anymore." His robe was made of spun gold. Thousands of people were greeting him. The rewards of missionaries are great, and God loves missions-minded people.

I was taken to one house on the street on which I was walking. It was a single mansion carved out of a single, giant pearl. The house seemed to be two hundred fifty to three hundred feet across and one hundred feet tall.

The furniture inside had been formed by angels who had molded and carved the pearl into shape. Even the chandelier had been carved out of the pearl, and it was lit. It glowed from within.

The house made of pearl belonged to a woman named Pearl, and the angels told me her story. She had been a missionary known for giving to the poor. Eventually, she had died of starvation. The house of pearl was a reward for a pure heart.

There were many different kinds of houses on this street. It would be unbelievable to consider building them in any place but heaven.

As I was passing by one street corner—whether I was walking or floating, I do not know, for an angel was holding me by the arm—I wanted to stop and see a specific mansion that belonged to another missionary. We stopped for a moment. It appeared to be made of solid gold, but there was wood, also. There were hundreds of people in this mansion. They were all people whom this missionary had led to the Lord. He had been a part of their families' lives. Now, they were still a part of his big family, and they were really joyous. The peace and tranquility there were unbelievable. As I walked by, they waved and called to me, saying, "Hello, Richard. It is good to see you." They knew me, but I didn't seem to know any of them—or remember knowing them.

Everybody in heaven is so friendly. People would often call from across the street, "Hello, Richard. How are you doing?"

"Where Thieves Do Not Break in and Steal"

There were also larger buildings on this street. Of all the buildings I saw in heaven, none of them had locks on the doors, and the doors were not closed. Whether they were mansions, smaller homes, or apartment buildings (yes, some people liked living in condominiums in heaven), all were open. Some had windows, but some did not. There are no storms and there are no thieves. *"Store up for yourselves treasures in heaven, where moth and rust do not destroy, and where thieves do not break in and steal"* (Matthew 6:20). Everyone who comes by is perfectly welcome to enter your house, whether you are there or not. But, out of respect, I don't believe anyone enters anyone else's home when the resident is not there.

Indescribable Architecture

I saw houses that were brightly lit from the inside and whose architecture was beautiful. In heaven, it seems that the architecture includes large pillars. Every home had large porches with pillars and huge archways. Some of the homes were made out of what seemed to be a type of brick or stone material. Others were made out of a type of wood. Yet, as I looked, there were no nails or even pegs. Not a piece was sawn, but everything was crafted and fit perfectly together. The fit was so perfect that no nails were needed. It was as if the houses had formed themselves into existence.

When I put my ear up to anything solid, I heard it humming the most beautiful songs.

I saw a veranda on one home that looked like it was made of onyx. You could see through it; it was as clear as glass. Inlaid in the porch were precious stones and gold and silver, and there were great diamonds (the things we hold so dear).

I saw several large cities in heaven, and each city had wide streets. One particular area I went to had seven huge, main streets that ran toward the Throne. The architecture there was extraordinary. I saw a home made of clear stone embedded with roses that were alive and growing and gave off the most beautiful aroma.

When I put my ear up to anything solid in heaven, I heard it humming the most beautiful songs. Some of the songs were ones we sing on earth, but others were not. Everything gave praise and glory to the Lord.

EVERYTHING ELSE DIMS AT THE SIGHT OF JESUS

Everything was so beautiful, but it all dimmed at the very sight of Jesus. Just one glimpse of Him, and everything else grew pale in comparison. When I saw Him and looked upon His wonderful face, even the beautiful architecture of heaven was forgotten. He is the express image of the Father (see Hebrews 1:3 KJV), and all of heaven revolves around the Lord and His great mercy.

> *He is the image of the invisible God, the firstborn over all creation. For by him all things were created: things in heaven and on earth, visible and invisible, whether thrones or powers or rulers or authorities; all things were created by him and for him. He is before all things, and in him all things hold together.*
>
> (Colossians 1:15–17)

THE CRYSTAL CITY OF LIGHTS

In the distance, I could hear beautiful chimes coming from across the crystal sea. It seemed as though it was so far away, yet it was an easy stroll for the inhabitants of this wonderful place called heaven.

I so wanted to see what was over there, and something seemed to be drawing me, but, for some reason better left to the Lord Jesus, I was not allowed to go. I asked why and received a stern glance. That was all I needed to know about that.

A place that I was allowed to see, which was not too distant, was a crystal city that appeared to be made wholly of lights. Each light was different—and glowing. The lights were giving off rays of glory that shone brighter than any earthly sun ever could.

It was as though the whole city was filled with tall buildings. Some were floating in the air. Some were round. One was shaped like a huge diamond; it alone was clearly visible to me, yet I was at least several miles away from it. It is very difficult to describe. It reminds me of the apostle Paul's experience: *"He heard inexpressible things, things that man is not permitted to tell"* (2 Corinthians 12:4). People continually came out from the city. I didn't know their purpose, and I was not going to ask—not this time.

> **There were chimes and a bell system playing such wonderful music.**

There were chimes and a bell system that was playing such wonderful music. I still remember the choirs of people and the angels who were singing from the heights above. I wept with adoration and joy at seeing and hearing these wonders that I found impossible to explain. Again, to truly describe them with mere earthly words completely fails me. Oh, that I could express what I felt, and what I now feel!

After the crystal city of lights, I was with Jesus most of the time.

MY OWN HEAVENLY HOME

I was taken to another home that was just off the main street on which I was walking. I was weeping with joy. I was joining in the joy and happiness of everybody. This home was not as big as some of the others, but it was a fine home. If it were possible to build on earth, it would cost probably a trillion dollars—again, if it were even possible to build. It was bigger than the White House. The angels told me I had to stop there, saying, "Somebody wants to talk to you."

I walked up to the house, and there was my grandfather, sitting on the front porch—and my grandmother was there, too. The house was their heavenly home! I remember falling down on my knees and saying, "Grandpa." When he stood up, I noticed that he looked like he was only in his late twenties or early thirties. When he'd died, he'd been ninety-seven.

Now, he was in perfect health, and so was Grandma. We hugged, and I just didn't know what to say. After a few moments, they said, "Richard, you have an appointment with God, but you will be back. Your home is just over yonder." They pointed down the street, where there was an open lot for a home to be built. I have never thought I have done anything to deserve all the goodness God has shown me, especially this. Suddenly, I was gone from them, but, supernaturally, I knew they were smiling. They knew what was going on. They had been told.

> *In heaven, I saw many mansions belonging to people I loved and who loved me.*

I saw many homes on that street for people whom I loved and who loved me. I saw some of the great generals in God's Army. I saw evangelist Jack Coe Sr. He wasn't sick, and he wasn't as heavy as he'd been on earth. He was standing in a crowd of people, teaching them with a loud, booming voice. He waved at me, and I waved back. There wasn't time to talk.

I also saw evangelist William Branham. He was sitting and talking with the Lord. I didn't want to interrupt him. He also gave me a wave, and I waved back. Jesus looked at me and smiled, and, again, supernaturally, I knew that He was saying, "Richard will be back; he is just visiting."

I saw other people who had died and had gone to be with Jesus. I saw great preachers from throughout the ages. They were out among the people, encouraging them, telling of the great wonders of heaven and the great things God had done for them. Some of the people had been there for a long time, but they were still learning. Just like little children, they were soaking up something they wanted badly to learn.

Then, the angel on the left said, "We have to go toward the Throne," and we were gone.

EVERYTHING FLOWS INTO AND OUT OF THE THRONE OF GOD

Everything in heaven flows into and out of the Throne. However you arrive there, all traffic moves toward the Throne: from the veil, in the beautiful conveyances, and coming down from the sky. In whatever way God brings you into heaven, you move toward the Throne.

People in heaven earnestly desire to get to the Throne and to talk to Jesus. They might be standing on a street corner looking down the street and see Jesus walking toward them. In wonderment, they exclaim, "He is coming! He is coming our way. We are going to get to talk to Him!"

Many times, I saw Jesus talking with people, and He would turn and look at me. I wanted to talk to Him, but I knew that I had to wait my turn. I felt great peace. When I saw Him, I always had a desire to go before God on the Throne.

THE TAPESTRY

I was walking down a beautiful street on my way to the Throne Room, which loomed so magnificently in the near distance. On my right, I noticed a wonder that, like everything else, took my breath away. There, in the large picture window of a beautiful home, was a sight that still makes me shout glory.

I was told to go inside the mansion and "behold God's glory."

A woman was weaving the most beautiful tapestry that I had ever seen. I was told to go inside the mansion and "behold

God's glory." The tapestry was hanging in midair without any visible means of support. I can't explain it. I can only tell you what I was shown.

The woman had a huge ball of yarn-like material, and she was speaking softly to it, telling it what she wanted it to be. Instantly, it obeyed her wishes. I noticed immediately the beautiful picture that was being formed in the finished part of the tapestry. I also saw that the tapestry was a picture of everything that was visible through the window of the mansion.

I was told that just as we are made in the image of God, the picture was being made in the image of what was going on outside the window. The image on the tapestry had depth, and it seemed as if you could have walked into it. Again, everything going on outside the window was going on in the tapestry. Some people were moving around and walking past the windows. Others were standing around in groups, singing. I could hear them, just as if I were standing right by the window. The leaves in the trees were moving as if a gentle breeze were blowing. I also saw myself, from just moments before. I was standing outside of the window, looking in. I asked one of the angels, "When did she weave this into the tapestry?"

He told me, "It was the day that you were born again." I was overtaken with emotion, and I wept.

"Come. You have an appointment with the God of your heritage."

I tried to speak, but again, I was speechless. The angel just smiled a kind, gentle smile, and I was made to know then about how the angels do rejoice at the moment that someone is born again. (See Luke 15:10.) They are created and empowered for just this very moment. Their highest joy is to serve God and to be on assignment where the Lord sends them. They weep with joy at the moment a person receives Christ as his or her Savior, and they go into action immediately. God has His will all planned out for us. We must follow Jesus. He never fails.

An Eternal Testimony Service

I was then taken to a large theater where a testimony service was going on. There were thousands there, and from what I was told, it would be going on for eternity. I heard thunderous shouting of praise and glory, and then I heard a very familiar voice. He was saying, "I was given a promise from the Lord regarding the life of my grandson, thirty-five years before he was born. I was told that he would be a blessing to his generation and that he would be used by God in a mighty way. He was a child preacher, and now he is here. Our God never fails." I looked around to see who he was talking about. Since I, also, had started very young in the ministry, I was excited about seeing this man. Was the voice talking about King David, or perhaps Samuel? Was I going to get to see Samuel? I found that I could see Samuel, so I shouted, "I want to see Samuel. Let me see this one who also loved God so much." Yet, I would not meet Samuel here.

I was led to an area that looked like a stage, and, as I looked up, there was my grandpa. He was the speaker! He pointed at me and said, "There he is now." I wept with joy at seeing him again, and I just fell on the marble floor. A hand picked me up. It was Grandpa's. Grandma was there, too, and also my grandpa's brothers, Lester and Marion. They had their families with them, and many more people whom I had never seen before. They would not come any closer, and I instinctively knew that God would not allow me to embrace them yet. Everyone was beaming with joy.

Then, I was instantly in another place. I was told, "Come, you have an appointment with destiny." I walked along, still overcome with joyful weeping and with the impact of what had just happened.

I saw a group of about fourteen warrior angels who were coming from the direction of the Throne. The angels were a good twenty feet tall and ten feet across at the shoulders. Their eyes glistened with a fiery light from the altars of God, and their swords were flames of fire. The ground shook as they passed by me.

"These warrior angels are being sent into your future for when you need them."

I stepped aside, and the angels with me bowed their heads in respect. I thought to myself, *I would never want to be any demon that tried to fight with them. Just one of them could destroy an entire army.*

Then, I heard that strong, firm, yet so gentle voice. Jesus was behind me. He said, "I wanted you to see them. They are being sent into your future. They will be there when you need them."

I was reminded of the Scripture, *"Are not all angels ministering spirits sent to serve those who will inherit salvation?"* (Hebrews 1:14).

Later in life, I would need them and would receive their help on several occasions—sometimes, in a very special, personal, and real way. Somehow, I knew that all these things were to prepare me for the future that God had in store for me. Again, I wept. The angels put their arms around me and said in unison, "And God has given His angels charge over you, to bear you up, lest at any time you should dash your foot against a stone." (See Psalm 91:11–12 KJV.)

I cried, "Glory to God!" with great joy.

I could see Jesus again, among His people, and there was a great throng of children surrounding Him. I heard Him say, "Look at this," as He threw a large ball of what looked like glory cloud into the air. When it reached about two thousand feet in the air, it exploded into a display that looked like the fireworks we are familiar with on earth, and with such a variety of colors. Yet, instead of fading away, it got bigger and bigger. Then, it took the shape of a tree and slowly floated to the ground. It was instantly rooted and began to grow. It looked similar to the other trees there. It was simply beautiful.

Jesus does only what is perfect. It is the law of heaven.

I remember all the people who were standing there, watching with great awe.

THE MARRIAGE SUPPER OF THE LAMB

Then, Jesus turned to me and said to the angels, "Take Richard to My marriage supper feast, and let him see it. It is almost ready." I was there before I could even think.

I saw a building that was very tall. It had arched supports and columns that were about fifty feet apart. The tables where the supper feast was to be held were made of gold and inlaid with jewels. These tables were lined with chairs that looked like kings' thrones. That is how they appeared to me, and I have no other words to explain the beautiful way they were constructed. The pavilion was about twenty miles long, in my best estimation. There were three rows of tables in a racking semicircle, with a throne in the background.

Each chair had a name engraved on the inside of the back. I asked when they had been engraved, and the Lord said, "When their names were recorded in the Lamb's Book of Life."

I grew silent and bowed my head with complete gratitude. Then, I raised my head and looked ahead of me. In that same instant, I saw my name engraved on one of the chairs. I wanted so much to sit in that chair, but Jesus said, "Not yet. It shall be sat in for the first time when My Father says, 'Sit at the marriage feast of My Son.' A virgin shall be given, and a virgin feast shall be given to a virgin Groom." And again, I wept with great joy.

> *Each chair at the marriage feast of the Lamb has a name engraved on it.*

There were goblets filled with sweet nectar from heaven. A golden dish was filled with heaven's best. Everything was prepared to perfection. The marriage supper was ready for the Groom to make His entrance. There was room enough for multiplied millions of people.

6

God Knows Our Tomorrows

*"In him we were also chosen, having been
predestined according to the plan of him who works
out everything in conformity with the purpose of his
will, in order that we, who were the first to hope in
Christ, might be for the praise of his glory."*

—Ephesians 1:11–12

I was taken into a very large building that had a huge archway. Inside were rows upon rows of shelves with books.
The shelves seemed to be miles long and miles high, and the
books looked about fifteen feet tall. There were hundreds of
angels servicing the books. They were going in and out—
there was a lot of activity.

THE ARCHIVES OF HEAVEN

God keeps records, and this large building was the
Archives of Heaven.

*And I saw the dead, great and small, standing before
the throne, and books were opened. Another book was
opened, which is the book of life. The dead were judged
according to what they had done as recorded in the
books.* (Revelation 20:12)

The Archives of Heaven contain the different books
about our lives, and these are the books that are taken to
God when judgment time comes. The books are the records

of our works here on earth. If a person sins, it is recorded in the book.

I was given the understanding that when we repent, anything that we have done that was wrong or sinful in nature and was recorded in the books is erased for eternity. No one can find the record, not even God.

I saw another very large building, different from the Archives. In that building is a book corresponding to every person on earth. There are other books about our lives, which are pictorial records. Every thought and every reaction—everything—is recorded in heaven.

There were many different books for each person. Tall, slender angels took care of the huge books. These angels appeared to be eight to nine feet tall, and they wrote in the books using a golden quill that was about five feet long and apparently could write forever. An angel would hold a book in his right hand and make the record with his left.

I saw angels pull out books with their left hands and open the thick pages. In each page was something like a video screen, except the images were three-dimensional. The images contained the history of life. And the books were written—the pictures were created—before time.

> *Your eyes saw my unformed body. All the days ordained for me were written in your book before one of them came to be.*   (Psalm 139:16)

GOD ORDERS OUR TOMORROWS BY OUR PRAYERS TODAY

God is able to go forward or backward in time. He created time; He invented it. God sets up our tomorrows because of our prayers and our seeking Him today. God knows what is coming tomorrow. He orders our tomorrows, but He orders them because we pray today. As we pray, God gives us our tomorrows by a system of weights and measures. In other words, we can know what is coming tomorrow because of the checks and balances in our spirits. The Holy Spirit speaks to our spirits and causes us to pray and to seek God. He also confirms His plans to us and gives us direction in life, telling us, "Yes," "No," or "Not yet."

Invariably, when we are praying about tomorrow or what is going to happen down the line, it is because God has a blessing in store for us and the devil wants to steal it away or trip us up. When we pray earnestly, it releases God to go into our tomorrows and lay a trap for the devil and make sure our blessings are there, right on time. This is something I was told by the Lord when I was in heaven.

I was also told that all of our tomorrows are God's yesterdays.

A LESSON ABOUT SEEKING GOD

I was taken to a place that I didn't understand at first. I was standing on the edge of the universe, and I saw all of the universe as a great spiral. From this vantage point, it looked like a huge, wound-up clock spring. The center was pure white, and the light got dimmer and dimmer as it got out to where I was, on the edge. I was closer to this than some of the other people were. I could see people way behind me, and they thought they were close. People up ahead of

Praying releases God to go into our tomorrows, lay a trap for the devil, and bring our blessings right on time.

me also thought they were close, but they were ahead of other people in time.

Then, I learned a lesson about seeking God. Men everywhere ought to seek God and be thankful for where they are with Him. Do not be envious of others who may be a little bit ahead, and pray for those who are behind you. All together, we form a group that is seeking God.

> *Let us not give up meeting together* [*"not forsaking the assembling of ourselves together"* KJV], *as some are in the habit of doing, but let us encourage one another— and all the more as you see the Day approaching.*
> (Hebrews 10:25)

The Word tells us not to forsake the assembling of ourselves together, and even more so as we see that the day of the Lord's return is fast approaching. There is strength in numbers, and when you are seeking God, the greater the anointing is, and the easier it is to pray. I learned this. God is way ahead of us because our tomorrows are God's yesterdays. He has already laid victory in our path. The Holy Spirit makes you aware (if you are really close to God) that you need to pray because there is something in your pathway you need to know about.

How many times has He done this for all of us? I don't know. I can tell you only about myself. Many times, He has, and I have always been better off praying about tomorrow knowing that God is there already. He is going to take care of me if I take special pains to pray *today*.

GOD CREATED OUR BLESSINGS BEFORE TIME BEGAN

The angels who were with me told me that some of the things I was seeing in heaven for myself were created by God before the beginning of time. Before He invented time, He finished heaven and the host of heaven, and He created the blessings I would need when I got there.

I was in a store that contained clothing that was exactly what I would require in heaven. I had my own section. God created everything that I would have need of in heaven before time was even created. He knew I would be there.

> *God created everything we would need in heaven before time was even created.*

Yet, even though certain things were made before time began, there were other places in heaven where I saw homes being built. There were angels at work, people busy at work, creating homes and putting blessings there that we couldn't receive on earth—blessings received in heaven.

7

The Library of God's Knowledge

*"Oh, the depth of the riches of the wisdom
and knowledge of God!"*

—Romans 11:33

A nother building I was taken to contained the written part of God's knowledge. God wrote some of His knowledge so that we would have something to relate to. There were individual symbols, each having the interpretation of the symbol written by God. When you are in the Library of God's Knowledge, your mind is automatically stimulated.

I talked with one man who was in this building, and he said, "Brother Richard, I have been here for two millennia, and I've only gotten to page two."

Millions of angels come and go from this library, as well as the same number of people of the inhabitants of heaven. These angels are on their way to earth. Many times in this life, we don't know what to do, and we pray for wisdom. Again, the Bible says that angels are ministers to the heirs of salvation. *"Are not all angels ministering spirits sent to serve those who will inherit salvation?"* (Hebrews 1:14). The Library of God's Knowledge is where the angels go to get wisdom. And we can receive it. Sometimes, it is brought directly by the Holy Spirit Himself. People in heaven have access to it and never forget.

There are great universities in heaven—I mean *great*—and there are many of them. Our education is not complete when we leave earth. We have only just begun.

I saw two giant buildings that were colleges for people. The people were taught by angels and other people. All subjects were taught, even singing. Every song, every note, every word you are taught stays with you throughout eternity. There is no end to learning. All of your mind is illuminated to the wisdom and knowledge of heaven. One hundred percent of your mind is used—and it is increasing in capability. You can do anything in heaven that your heart desires to do because your desire is for the things that are right.

In heaven, your whole mind is illuminated to God's wisdom and knowledge.

The university buildings appeared to be a mile or two long and a mile or two deep. They were great buildings with the capacity to hold hundreds and hundreds of thousands of people. The classrooms were huge auditoriums. I could see them through the windows as I walked by. People were learning and praising God inside. And I was told that anything you learn in heaven, you never forget.

I remember standing for just a moment in utter amazement. I could hear everything that was said. People were praising God, and many secrets of God were being made known.

8
Memorials

*"That the grace that is reaching more and
more people may cause thanksgiving to
overflow to the glory of God."*

—2 Corinthians 4:15

On my tour, I was taken to a building that looked like a huge, layered wedding cake. The bottom layer, which was big and round, was about fifteen feet tall. It had a lit archway, and above the archway was a name. I went in.

Inside were walls on which revival scenes were being played over and over. These were the revivals I had been involved with since I was a child. God was continually getting the glory as they were displayed over and over.

In three-inch letters, it was written:

THE GLORY GOD GETS OUT OF RICHARD'S LIFE

I saw other memorials. In the memorial of Cornelius, the centurion mentioned in Acts 10 who was generous toward the poor and needy, there was much almsgiving. His memorial looked a lot like the Washington Monument, but not as tall. It had writing on it, and angels were standing there making announcements about the almsgiving that Cornelius had done. It was a place where people came to see what was mentioned in the Bible. I never saw Cornelius, and I don't know what he looked like, but I felt in my spirit that he wasn't very far away. He was talking with people and giving God the glory.

There were more memorials everywhere. Each memorial depicted some great victory that one of God's children had won down here on earth. Memorials told when someone—a very bad sinner—came to Christ. Memorials told when some great battle was fought and won for the glory of God's Spirit. I saw a memorial about a service that Billy Graham had held in Southern California. It told about the glory that God had received there and the number of people who had been saved, and the words were sealed in God forever.

I saw other memorials. It was a glorious place to be. I saw Smith Wigglesworth's memorial. I did not get to talk with him because he was at a distance, but he looked my way and smiled, waving his hand. He was busy directing people here and there and telling them how much God loved them and what He had in store for them in heaven.

He was busy telling people how much God loved them and what He had in store for them in heaven.

Smith Wigglesworth was doing in heaven what he had done on earth: helping people. Since there are no sick people in heaven for him to pray for, he was talking with all the new arrivals who had read his books and heard him speak and wanted to talk to him. But he was very humble going about his business of helping others.

The greatest among you will be your servant.

(Matthew 23:11)

He who would be the greatest among you, let him be the servant of all. (See Matthew 20:27.) That is one of the rules that heaven is run by. You are a servant of all; you are a servant to all; and you are a servant of the Lord. The way to "go up" with God is to "go down" and get beyond yourself to where there is nothing of you left. The death of self is worth much in the sight of God.

I was told by the angels who were with me that there are things that God highly prizes: He highly prizes someone who is absolutely truthful and totally honest, who prays before he makes any decision, and who makes sure that all his decisions are what God wants him to make. God highly prizes someone who will pray and seek Him in all things and be obedient. Above all is obedience to God. Those are principles that heaven is run by.

THE WAY OF THE ROSE

I was taken to an avenue named The Way of the Rose. I somehow knew that there were important and long-lasting events connected with this avenue. I asked the angel on my left if he would tell me why I was here at this beautiful place. He replied, "It is for you to obey, not to question God." He spoke with a stern voice, so that settled that. There were some homes still under construction. One of them had names carved in beautiful letters above the entrance. These names were Paul and Judy of the family Hegstrom. At that time, I didn't know who they were, and I didn't have the nerve to ask.

I noticed that the other homes were of similar construction. They were all joined together by beautiful, turf-green yards, with flowering trees that were thousands of feet tall. All of them were made so that the back and the front looked very much the same.

In addition, all of the houses were three stories tall. They had many spacious rooms, decorated with rose colored woodwork, and the rooms were filled with exquisite furniture. It all looked as though it was taken right out of

Buckingham Palace in London. In the backyards, there were many sitting areas with golden furniture, which, again, looked much like wrought-iron lawn furniture. The seat cushions were made out of spun gold.

> *It all looked as though it was taken right out of Buckingham Palace in London.*

Behind the homes was a large lake, as well as ornamental, hand-carved scenes of heaven. These scenes had live figures that moved and talked but remained part of the scene. They were carved out of a wood-like substance. Again, I cannot explain it. I can say only that this is what I was shown. The laws of physics that apply on earth did not apply there.

The main libraries in these houses were lined with books that were embossed with gold. They were heaven's pre-copies of books that have been written and that will be written in the time to come.

Of the library at the Hegstrom home, Jesus said to me, "These books were written by My Spirit at the beginning of time. They were given to Paul Hegstrom to write on earth when he was there. You will meet him later. When you do, tell him that there is much to do and not to slacken the pace." Then, Jesus said, "I will tell you more later."

Every member of a family was represented by his or her own home. Some of those members were already there. On the front of the Hegstrom home was a memorial to the glory that God had received from the yielded life of this man. Again, I was made to know that I would meet him later, in his season. I wept in praise and gratitude, and the angels began to praise God.

"Where the Roses Never Fade"

This incident will not mean as much to you as it did to me. I still get all emotional when I remember it. It brings to mind an evangelist friend of mine who was somewhat like a father to me. He would always sing this song for me: "Where the Roses Never Fade." I never have quite gotten over his sudden death.

The people all around me grew very quiet, and I felt that a very special moment was about to happen. I was aware of someone coming my way. I recognized him as an old friend who had been killed in a car accident many years ago. I was astonished to see him there. I was not aware that he had been converted. Once again, I was at a loss for words.

What a glad reunion day we will have in glory!

9

Music, Languages, and Clothing in Heaven

"Then I heard every creature in heaven and on earth and under the earth and on the sea, and all that is in them, singing: 'To him who sits on the throne and to the Lamb be praise and honor and glory and power, for ever and ever!'"

—Revelation 5:13

God does not want to lose one bit of the talent and skill that people have developed on earth. As I wrote before, when that talent is brought to heaven, it is multiplied a millionfold.

MUSIC EVERYWHERE

I saw and heard Johann Sebastian Bach on a huge organ that had notes below and above what people normally hear on earth; and I heard all of it. As he played, the choirs of heaven joined in praise and worship—everyone joined in the music.

I noticed something else in heaven: music was everywhere. People in the various villages and cities were praising God in song. One village would sing one song. Another village would sing a different song. As I went up in the air, I could hear music from the different villages at the same time, yet they were all singing in concert! The higher I went, the more villages I could hear, yet everyone seemed to be singing the same song in perfect harmony. I thought of it as "the song of heaven."

I saw choirs from a distance. Then, I saw them closer. I had heard them in the background, and I had also seen smaller groups singing. Sometimes, the choirs were groups of angels. Apparently, one of the songs was specifically for me. While I was there, I knew what it was. Now, I do not understand the song or its meaning, nor do I remember the melody or lyrics. It was for me to know only while I was there.

I understood that the songs the angels sang had something to do with ministry and something to do with what God was saying to people in heaven.

The songs that people sang were different. Sometimes, groups were made up of two or three people. Sometimes, there were large groups. I saw a large group in the setting of an amphitheater, and they seemed to be standing on air, even though it also looked like risers. They were singing songs similar to what we sing here on earth.

One song I remember is "The King Is Coming." But the title was slightly different: "The King Has Come." They went through the whole story from heaven's point of view, and it was a most beautiful song. I remember hearing it, but now I can't recall all the words.

When you leave heaven, you lose the ability to understand some of the things that you heard spoken there. Much of it you don't remember because you don't have earthly words to express it.

The closer I came to the Throne of God, the greater the number of people there were in the choirs. I remember a choir of what seemed to be fifty or sixty thousand. (While I was there, I knew the exact number, but now I don't remember.) They sang with the deepest bass and the highest soprano—beyond the ranges of anyone on earth. They could be heard pleasantly in the background all over heaven. It was music in the language of God.

HEAVENLY AND HUMAN LANGUAGES

In heaven, you can speak in a heavenly language anytime you want, and the people there can understand you completely.

> *In heaven, you seem to have the ability to speak all human languages, in addition to heaven's own language.*

I heard a language that sounded like Russian spoken by certain groups of people, yet other people whom I knew were not Russian could walk up to them and speak perfectly in that dialect. These people also spoke in a heavenly dialect, and they spoke perfect English, as well. It seems that in heaven, you have the ability to speak all human languages, in addition to heaven's own language.

HEAVENLY GARMENTS

There are stores in heaven, but they are unique stores aimed specifically at whoever walks through the door. There was a jewelry store with diamonds that represented a specific woman in a man's life. Again, one store I walked into had only suits and robes tailored specifically to my taste. In another store, I saw garments that had been made before the beginning of time. These had been put on the shelf and were in pristine condition, as if they had just been placed there.

Of course, no one would disturb them because they were for someone else. It is for your joy to make sure that others receive what God has for them.

I saw what seemed to be a gathering place—like a community center. Thousands of women were sitting at tables and benches in a parklike setting. In the center of them was a pile of beautiful clothing. They were sewing but did not have needles and thread in their hands. They were just putting pieces of cloth together and telling them what to be. The cloths became what the women said. The women were making garments for people who were soon to be there.

I believe that the garments were rewards that were being heaped up in heaven. In heaven, God rewards us for what we give on earth that is known only to Him. He knows what we give in secret. I saw this.

> *But when you give to the needy, do not let your left hand know what your right hand is doing, so that your giving may be in secret. Then your Father, who sees what is done in secret, will reward you.*
>
> (Matthew 6:3–4)

Dress in heaven varied. Some people were dressed in some sort of pants and pullover shirts that were pure white. One outfit I saw was bright yellow, but I saw others of different colors. I saw people dressed in suits similar to what we wear here on earth but much more expensive looking. I also saw people dressed as one would think angels would dress— in long, flowing robes. Clothing was made out of heavenly material.

I saw the Lord many times. He had gold around the ends of His sleeves and around His collar. He also had a golden waistband and gold around the hem of His long, flowing robe.

I cannot put into words how beautiful it was to see all these different people with their fabulous adornments. It was because of the anointing. Nowhere did I see people wearing jewelry; it wasn't necessary. The glow of God's presence just makes a person beautiful.

"I want to see God," I heard myself say. The angel corrected me, "No. You have an appointment." Angels do not go before God unless they are bidden.

—— 10 ——

Balconies and Chimes in Heaven

"Since we are surrounded by such a great cloud of witnesses, let us throw off everything that hinders and the sin that so easily entangles, and let us run with perseverance the race marked out for us."

—Hebrews 12:1

BALCONIES OVERLOOKING EARTH

I walked by groups and groups of people, and I could hear them talking. It was like the buzzing and busyness of people waiting at an airport or a train station. They were obviously waiting for someone. They were preparing something, also.

"We did this because we knew he would like it."

"Wait until he sees this."

It became obvious that these people were involved in the preparation of a mansion for a family member or friend. They were talking about this person who was about to arrive. Oh, the excitement they showed in anticipation of someone coming home! As I said earlier, there were announcement centers letting people know when a loved one was coming to heaven. These centers looked like band shells, except that they were made out of glory clouds. They were solid, yet you could see through them, and they seemed as if they lit up from the inside with a great amount of the glory that permeated everywhere. It was all different colors, like fire shooting through it: amber and gold. There were sparkles and an aroma—the fragrance of God.

At this band shell, someone was announcing a homecoming. There were a great number of people in the crowd, and, supernaturally, I knew it was a pastor coming home after many years of service to his church. He was on the way to the announcement center. He had already come through the veil, and there was great joy and wonderment in the people.

Again, there are balconies and bleachers in heaven that look over the events on earth. People come to watch prayers come to pass. They are the *"cloud of witnesses"*:

> *Therefore, since we are surrounded by such a great cloud of witnesses, let us throw off everything that hinders and the sin that so easily entangles, and let us run with perseverance the race marked out for us.*
>
> (Hebrews 12:1)

People in heaven watch births and weddings on earth. They are a cheering section, hollering out encouragement to us.

Diamond-like and Multicolored Chimes

I was shown chimes in heaven that were very loud and beautiful. They looked like diamonds and were about fifteen feet in either direction. They were suspended from a pole that was solid diamond and about five hundred feet tall. Nobody had to ring the chimes. Angels would rub them, and they would chime for what seemed like twenty minutes. As they chimed, people would join in with them, singing.

The chimes were like a huge minaret; they were tree-like and were everywhere. The pipes of the chimes were huge and had a deep, full sound that filled the air with harmonies that you could hear at a great distance. I was told that whenever someone got saved, the chimes made a sound.

At one time, I found myself hundreds—perhaps, even thousands—of feet in the air while being shown around heaven. Being high up and looking down, I could see many chimes. They were multicolored. Some of the chimes had glory coming out of them. They were like the crystal Diadem tree and gave off a wavering sound that was beautiful. It was like an organ playing continually. Whenever somebody got saved, they would chime a loud and beautiful song.

> *Whenever somebody got saved, a beautiful song would chime.*

I also saw chimes near the balconies of heaven. There were seven large towers there with chimes hanging from them. The saints of God would go to the balconies and begin to pray and worship God. Looking down on earth, they could see their promises coming to pass. Or, they would look in on a revival meeting, as they often did; they would say, "Preach it, preacher." They would join in with the service, and the chimes behind them would begin to give off the most beautiful, heavenly sound—a song of worship and praise.

Here on earth, there have been times in revival services when we have heard the anthems of glory being sung and the beautiful music in heaven playing along. From what I saw during my time in heaven, I believe we heard the chimes that were near the balconies of heaven. In those services, our praise and worship reached high enough to commingle with those that were coming down from heaven. Then there was a steady flow of God's Spirit. Oh, to be set in high places with Christ Jesus! We can experience being set in those heavenly places if we pay the price to stay in the Spirit of God. That is what this Scripture means:

> [God] *hath raised us up together, and made us sit together in heavenly places in Christ Jesus.*
>
> (Ephesians 2:6 KJV)

HEAVENLY REWARDS DEPARTMENT

The angel who accompanied me on my right told me about a rewards department in heaven. I did not see it, and I did not go there. It was explained to me, however, and I heard others talking about it.

It is a huge records building. This is where records are kept of the rewards that we do not receive on earth for some reason or other. An example would be the reward for giving to others or almsgiving to the Lord. Because of the love and compassion we have in our hearts, we give to the greater need. What we give here, we will receive back in heaven.

I was taken to a large building—large even by heaven's standards. There were many rooms inside, and the rooms were beautifully decorated. The furniture was extraordinary—beyond description. I saw what looked like a chair similar to a recliner. I didn't get to sit in it, but I saw someone else sit in it. As he did, the chair molded itself around him, providing tremendous comfort.

A book was given to him, and he began to read out loud to others around him. I don't know what he was reading—I wasn't allowed to hear it—but everyone was smiling and praising God. I really felt that within this book contained the desires, wants, and wishes of a Christian man here on earth. Plans were being laid according to what was written in the book. In the ways he had been a blessing to others, he was going to be blessed in heaven. And they were planning the home in which he was going to live in heaven. They were planning the heavenly events in store for him. God had made it known and had it written in this book.

I believe that the good things you make happen to others on earth will happen to you in heaven. In this one building—in this one room—were the intentions of God for the works of one man and how God was going to bless him. The building reflected the fact that God desires to bless us even more than we desire to receive from Him.

There were other rooms in this huge building. The rooms were mammoth, sometimes beyond description in size. Some of the rooms had huge chandeliers hanging from the ceilings. There were three chandeliers in the first room where the man was sitting in the chair. Each one was several hundred feet across. All three chandeliers were doing the same thing at the same time.

> *God desires to bless us even more than we desire to receive from Him.*

There was no electricity, but they glowed beautifully; they were lit with a glow from within. Like the Diadem tree, they continually glowed in different colors with what were almost like bursts of fire. They glowed and gave off energy. The energy seemed to go through everything in heaven. I believe it was the Shekinah glory of God. The Lamb—Jesus—is the light: the power and presence of God.

And the city had no need of the sun, neither of the moon, to shine in it: for the glory of God did lighten it, and the Lamb is the light thereof.

(Revelation 21:23 KJV)

All through this huge room, people were reading to others out of books and making plans. I heard one person say, "Now, let's do this." As he made a gesture in the air, arcs of what looked like fire sprang off of his hand, and they sparked like fireworks that hung in the air for a few moments. I thought, *Wow, I wish I could do that.*

One of the angels who stood by me heard my thoughts and said that in heaven, you have the ability to do things that you can't even think of on earth. You can do them in heaven because it pleases God. In heaven, the laws that govern earth are done away with, and the laws of heaven govern everything. And that's all he said about it.

> *In heaven, you have the ability to do things that you can't even think of on earth.*

I realized that anything that is possible in heaven and that gives glory, honor, and praise to the Lord can be a reward for things done on earth, especially in this room. I was also told that those who don't seek rewards on earth receive the biggest rewards in heaven. The people in this room were planning others' rewards from books that were spoken, written, and recorded by the Lord.

There were many other rooms, but I was not allowed to go into them. The gentle reminder was always there: "You have an appointment with God." I had to stick to the path. The angel would say, "No, you must be about the Father's business."

I really wanted to see this other large building because I somehow knew that it contained all the miracles that we need on earth for our bodies. I don't know the heavenly law concerning it, but I do know that God created everything we have need of for our bodies. In this and other large buildings, there appeared to be great factories. I don't know what was done in them. There were no smokestacks, power lines, or power plants. Only worship and praise came from them. I could hear it. And there were lots of people coming and going in and out of the buildings.

For a "factory," the architecture was beautiful: spires, arched doorways, and columns all around. This was the typical architecture of heaven. Off in the distance, I could see the Temple of God, or Throne Building, the biggest and most beautiful building in heaven. Every time I would look in its direction, something would stir within me: "I have an appointment with God."

——11——
Jesus Came My Way

"Your love, O LORD, reaches to the heavens, your
faithfulness to the skies. Your righteousness is like the
mighty mountains, your justice like the great deep....
How priceless is your unfailing love! Both high and
low among men find refuge in the shadow of your
wings. They feast on the abundance of your house; you
give them drink from your river of
delights. For with you is the fountain of life;
in your light we see light."

—Psalm 36:5–9

There were fountains everywhere in heaven. *Where did the water come from?* I wondered. Some of the fountains were the size of a city block. You could see right through some of them; they looked like ice but were a kind of crystal. The figures in them were "alive"—they moved.

FOUNTAINS WITH MOVING STATUES AND COLORFUL WATER

The seemingly thousands of fountains in heaven depict different things. One that I saw had a statue of Jesus pouring out a large pitcher of glory. The glory was falling on little children and grown-ups who had their hands up, wanting a drink. Again, the statues were somehow alive, for they moved, yet they were made out of stone. I could see Jesus

Himself in the distance and the image of Him moving in a fountain right in front of me. *How does stone live?* I thought. Jesus looked at me and smiled.

At another fountain, hundreds of people were standing around, watching. The water turned hundreds of different colors and flowed down over a beautiful mountain with trees. The water shot into the air and came down in a mist over it.

The mist clung to the trees as tinsel does on a Christmas tree. It sparkled. Yet the trees on the mountain were the most vivid green and other colors. The water wasn't like the water we have here on earth—and yet it was. It was water, but it could do anything you wanted it to do. It turned into ice that was not cold. There were sheets of ice on the trees that were dazzling.

I could not tell where the water drained. There were no pipes in the ground. There was apparently no need for plumbing. There are no bathrooms; none of the houses I saw in heaven had bathrooms. You don't have to eat in heaven, and, if you did eat, you wouldn't have to go to the bathroom, anyway. You don't even need to take baths in heaven.

Similarly, there is no electric current, but there are lights everywhere, including big chandeliers. Nothing in heaven casts a shadow—the light is even from every direction. Just as there are no tangible shadows in heaven, there are no emotional or spiritual ones, either. There is no variableness, no shadow of failing. Things cannot fail in heaven. They are set for eternity.

Every good and perfect gift is from above, coming down from the Father of the heavenly lights, who does not change like shifting shadows.   (James 1:17)

The closer I got to the Throne, the greater were the wonders.

"TELL MY PEOPLE I LOVE THEM"

I saw Jesus coming my way. I stopped, and the angels stood at attention and backed away from me a couple of feet. Then, they bowed low, backed up, and stood at attention again with looks of adoration on their faces. Jesus walked in my direction, and I fell on my face like a dead man. He stopped a few feet from me, and I remember looking at the nail holes through His feet. They shone with a light from the inside of beautiful, beautiful Jesus. He suffered this for me! I had no words.

Evidently, He touched me, and I was able to stand. I did not feel worthy to stand or to look at His face. He reached out His fingers, lifted my chin, and said, "Son, look at Me. I love you. Even though you have been disobedient and haven't done what I have told you to do, I still love you, and I desire for you to tell My people about this place called heaven. I desire for you to tell My people the glorious things that My Father has made for them, that they might want to come here. I have chosen you and ordained you for this one work above all others that I might speak to you on this day of these things."

"Tell My people about this place called heaven and the glorious things that My Father has made for them."

He took my hand and began to walk with me like a father would with a little child. We walked a little further down the street, and He said, "I have many things to tell you. I will come to you again in just a short time. I have something else to tell you, but right now, there is more for you to see. More for you to witness and experience. Tell My people I am coming soon. I love them." Then, He gave me a big hug and kissed me on the cheek and said, "I love you, too."

He held out His hands in front of me, and I saw the nail scars. The wounds were open, shining with a beautiful light. I saw my name written in His hand, looking almost as if a knife had carved it there.

"See," He said, "your name is carved in My hand." I knew then what that Scripture meant:

See, I have engraved you on the palms of my hands; your walls are ever before me.   (Isaiah 49:16)

Then, He looked at me again and said, "I have more to tell you later." Again, He said this. And He said, "Go with the angels. They are going to take you to see more people and to see more things. I have an appointment, and I have to go. My Father wants me; I must go. I am always obedient to My Father." Suddenly, He was gone. He just vanished out of sight and was gone. In a fraction of a moment, I saw Him off in the distance walking and talking with people going toward the Throne.

Then the angels came back around me.

THE FOUNTAIN OF ALL PEACE

Throughout this wonderful experience in heaven, I felt a peace and tranquility such as no human on earth has ever known. Ever.

Several times, I glimpsed in the distance what I would call a mountain-sized fountain. There are no adequate words to describe it, but I will try. The fountain was very high: it appeared to be about ten miles in circumference at the base. At the top was another living statue of Jesus. He had an altar cup in His hands and was lifting it up before the Throne of God, which was in the distance. His hands were extended toward the Throne of God, and the vessel He held up was overflowing with what appeared to be the living blood of our Savior, which was shed on Calvary's hill. He was standing above the fountain, suspended in midair.

A duplicate of the cross of Calvary was there, too. Jesus was not on it; He was the Master of it. Below Him and the cross of Calvary were seven layers of scenes carved into the stone, which was pure white, almost transparent, and alive.

The scenes were about the price paid at Calvary and the redemption of the lost souls. In the lower layers were scenes that told the redemptive story of mankind. Again, the carved scenes were alive and were playing over and over the complete life of Christ on earth. I can't explain it any better than this. I can tell you only what I was shown.

The blood pouring out of the altar cup became a torrent of pure, crystal clear water that seemed to be alive. It sparkled like jewels in the sun. There was a glory cloud of—I was told—the peace of God. It was the peace of His presence, which surpassed all understanding. (See Philippians 4:7.) It was the third most beautiful and glorious place in heaven.

There was a glory cloud of the peace of God's presence, which surpassed all understanding.

The first most glorious place I saw was God's Throne, with God sitting upon it.

The second, and equal to it, was the Lord Jesus.

The third was the fountain of all peace.

There were what seemed like millions of people simply shining in its glory. The glory of it reached to all of heaven, and to all existence. In times of trouble, I think about the fountain of God's peace, and I am totally at peace once again.

Again, there are no words to properly explain it, even though I experience it all, over and over again.

THE LIVING ARK OF THE COVENANT

I was told that I was expected at the meeting place. The angels seemed anxious for me to get there. There was an excitement that was vibrating all over my body.

I noticed that the people around me were as excited about it as I was, way down deep inside. It was an awesome feeling. I wondered what I was going to see there.

Then, Jesus was there again, and He said to the angels, "Take him by the way of the living ark." And as fast as the blink of an eye, we were there.

I found myself standing in front of a raised platform, with an exact duplicate of the original ark of the covenant. Another living statue of Christ was suspended above the ark, with His precious blood dripping down on the area around the ark. Nothing else needed to be said. I was weeping with gratitude, and thousands of others were doing the same. It is a living memorial to the love of God.

THE MEETING PLACE

From my seventh birthday on, my life has been a series of experiences with God. I will never really know why God chose me, for I am the most ordinary man you have ever seen. It was simply the will of God for my life. I have met men and women of God who have had similar experiences, and they didn't understand why they were chosen, either. God alone knows.

On earth, I had experienced a very powerful encounter with God in which I was caught away to heaven, where I received supernatural peace. That experience of peace was about to be repeated.

Yet, first, I was taken to a wooded area, which was some distance from the City of God. It was in the beautiful countryside, about a mile from any houses. All along the street where we walked through this wooded area, hundreds of people were having joyful reunion parties. There were tears of joy flowing from every eye.

I noticed that some of the people were stopping, looking toward me, and saying, "There is brother Richard." I had the feeling that we had met, perhaps in a revival meeting somewhere. So, I waved to them and said, "God bless you."

A little boy of about six years old ran up to me and hugged me. He said, "Do you remember me?" I didn't remember at first, but then it came to me. God had suddenly put it in my mind. The angels smiled, and the angel who did the talking said, "The boy was a crippled child who could walk after prayer."

"Yes," I said. "I remember now."

The boy said, "I just got here. Jesus came and got me just now. See, I am not sick anymore."

People began to shout, "Glory," and it made me think of the excitement on earth when a revival is about to break out.

"I will see you later," the boy said as he ran off toward a group of children who were playing nearby.

I was taken to an amphitheater. Inside, there were seats along one side. Then, up to the ceiling, it was like a movie theater. Where the stage would have been, there was a window that reached from the floor clear up to the ceiling and from one side of the building to the other. You could look out over all of heaven—it was breathtaking.

Everyone sat in complete, silent adoration of God while waiting for someone to speak to them. I was told to be silent, as none may speak there. To behold the beauty of heaven seemed to be the purpose of all who were sitting there. I was told that this is the meeting place. This is where all the cares that people had on earth are cleansed away. Everyone leaves there having had his or her first encounter with the cleansing of heaven's glory.

The heavenly "meeting place" is where all the cares that people had on earth are cleansed away.

Then, I was aware of why I had been brought here before. When it had happened earlier, while I was still on earth, I had been in a war with the evil one. Here, I had felt a peace and quietness that had made the problem I'd been facing just melt away. I fell on my face, and my spirit within me cried, *Holy, holy, holy.* It was *"joy unspeakable and full of glory"* (1 Peter 1:8 KJV).

12

The City of God

"Glorious things are said of you, O city of God."

—Psalm 87:3

I had been walking on the pathway up to this point, though I had seen other people floating. Now, something really different happened to me—I myself went up. I was going up through what looked like clouds, but they were actually groups of people. I could see the entire city. The higher I got, the more of heaven I could see, and it was a busy, busy place. In the distance, I could see the Throne of God.

MOUNTAINS WITH SNOW AND TERRACED PARKS

There were mountains that had to be fifty thousand feet tall. They had snow that never melted, even though the temperature was always just right. I was taken to the base of a mountain.

The mountains were covered with terraced parks. I noticed what I was told were "conveyances." These conveyances floated like boats in the sky. They were made of carved wood and metal. People sat in them and talked with each other as they floated around. In them, angels minister blessing to the people traveling together.

THE SEA OF GOD'S GLORY

I was taken to the ocean, the Sea of God's Glory. It was crystal clear and seemed to have no bottom in places.

There were what seemed like millions of people in the water and under the water. As I said before, no one could drown, and people were playing under the water. One man had built a castle out of rocks on the bottom of the ocean.

In heaven, there are conveyances on the oceans, the seas, and the four major rivers, just as there are in the air. They are like boats in the water. Some are very large. Some are hand carved with biblical sayings on them. Some are guided by angels. There are also land conveyances, which travel on golden roads. They seem to exist so that people can sit and enjoy each other's companionship. It was as if these vehicles were the pastime building projects of someone who enjoyed making conveyances.

HEAVEN'S CAPITAL CITY

From up in the air, I could see the City of God. I had seen other cities in heaven. For example, I had been shown an oasis that is a city on a peninsula extending out into the ocean. Yet the City of God appeared to be heaven's capital city. It was built around the Throne and contained what looked like beautiful apartment buildings. I saw a waterfall coming off of one building. There were villages in the countryside surrounding the City of God. They appeared to be hundreds of miles from the outskirts of the city. These villages were of many different styles, just as there are around the world today. But all were clean and beautiful, with flowing fountains everywhere. I saw buildings suspended in the air thousands of feet above the ground. This is when I floated high in the air and heard the villages singing their songs in perfect harmony.

LAYERS OF HEAVEN

It seemed as though heaven was layered. There was a layer with an atmosphere and thousands of feet of air, and then there was another layer with an atmosphere and thousands of feet of air. I don't know how big it was. I was taken up to an altitude of what seemed like thirty to forty thousand feet, and yet it was just a skip in the air.

In heaven, you can travel anywhere in moments of time.

In heaven, you can travel anywhere in moments of time. You can take a leisurely stroll to the layers just by walking through the air.

JESUS AT THE AUDITORIUM

Wherever I went, angels and people were around. Sometimes, just a few; sometimes, large groups. They were standing around talking with great joy and worshipping. At times, they were laughing with hilarious joy, evidently over a loved one coming home or a promise that had come to pass. And they were always talking about Jesus. I can still see Him going here and there among the people.

There was an auditorium that was an announcement center. The Lord Himself was on stage there. He was with me, but also, I could look down and see Him as He was with groups of people walking through the air. In heaven, Jesus is omnipresent. And instantly, at the right moment, He was on the stage of that auditorium, which seemed to have seated ten million people. I looked, and He was there, always, and right now.

The stage was beautiful. There was a throne on it, and I believe that it was where Jesus was sitting before He suddenly stood. There was no pulpit, but there was an area that was both gold and silver and had precious jewels. There was a fragrance—an aroma that was indescribable and beyond measure—the fragrance of God Himself.

The auditorium was open to the sky. In addition to the stage, there were bleachers and beautiful, hand-carved seats that were unbelievably comfortable to sit in. Anything you sit on in heaven is comfortable forever.

Again, the Lord suddenly was there on the stage of gold, ivory, silver, and a material I didn't recognize. I was given the understanding that there are other theaters throughout heaven where announcements are made. But this was the theater where Jesus announced that He was going to be born of a virgin.

Someplace in heaven, there is a reenactment of the manger scene and the virgin birth to the glory of God—an eternal nativity that declares the miracle: God became man.

Someplace in heaven, you can feel and hear the throbbing heart of God, loving, yearning, churning—you can feel His deep, loving compassion. He will do everything in His Word that He has promised. The sacrifice of His Son indicates that He was and is willing to do everything to redeem us.

> *You can feel God's deep, loving compassion. He will do everything in His Word that He has promised.*

He who did not spare his own Son, but gave him up for us all—how will he not also, along with him, graciously give us all things?   (Romans 8:32)

We often think that what is contained in the Word is the sum total of what God will do for us, but it is not. In a sense, God limited Himself when He recorded His Word for us. He didn't include all that He is and all that He can do, because He is infinite. While we are on earth, we cannot comprehend or receive what He has planned for us ultimately. We cannot fathom the capacity of God, but in heaven there are no limits.

> *Now to him who is able to do immeasurably more than all we ask or imagine, according to his power that is at work within us, to him be glory in the church and in Christ Jesus throughout all generations, for ever and ever! Amen.* (Ephesians 3:20–21)

In heaven, there is no yesterday and no tomorrow; there is only "right now." The right-now situation needed Jesus there in the auditorium, and that is where He was. He walked onstage to thunderous praise, worship, and adoration that seemed to go on forever. It was glorious.

Jesus stood there and looked at the people so lovingly. It was wonderful how He just looked at them and loved them. You could feel the Shekinah glory love that came out of Him. It was awesome. Once again, words fail.

Slowly, the people quieted down, and a holy hush came over the auditorium. Jesus was about to speak. Suddenly, He began to speak in a deep, bass voice—the sound I have heard so often—like rushing waters, metallic. (See Ezekiel 43:2; Revelation 1:15.) I do not know now what He said; I was not allowed to remember it. But I do know the topic was eternity and what it means to God and what God has in store for His people. It was awesome.

──13──
Mysteries of God

"How unsearchable [God's] *judgments, and his paths beyond tracing out! Who has known the mind of the Lord? Or who has been his counselor?"*

—Romans 11:33–34

As you might imagine, I had many questions. There were things I wanted to know. For example, I saw other levels of heaven that I didn't understand. When we started floating up into the sky, another level of heaven appeared with ground, buildings, and sky. But I couldn't see it from the first level.

OTHER LANDS, OCEANS, AND SEAS

Supernaturally, I knew that there were other continents, islands, freshwater oceans, and seas far away. The seas are large bodies of water surrounded by land but open to the oceans. I was not allowed to know anything about them, but I knew they existed. To me, heaven seemed like a very large planet—millions of times the size of Earth. Things there were tangible but not physical.

INFINITE LAYERS

If heaven is a planet, then it's God's personal planet. And if heaven is God's personal planet, then it is multilayered, as I mentioned before. No matter where I was, however, I could see the Throne of God, off in the distance. It's the very center of the universe, the center of all existence. That's where everything began. It is awesome.

I saw only four of these layers, but they seemed to go on to infinity. How big is God, and how big is His universe! There are vast places in heaven where people will never go or see.

ADDITIONAL QUESTIONS

For some reason, I could talk to only a few people. There were streets that I wanted to walk down in order to look at other things, but I was not allowed. There were buildings that I couldn't enter. I was told that there were some buildings people would never be allowed into.

Again, I marveled at the children. They were so advanced and yet still children. Apparently, even in heaven, people grow at different rates.

I wondered where the lumber came from for the buildings because no tree has ever been cut in heaven. Who made the bricks? What was made in the factories? They were huge.

I learned that the Diadem trees were made before the creation of the earth. I thought to myself that I could find out how old the earth is by asking how old the Diadem trees are. That was to remain a mystery—I was not allowed to know. But they were miles in diameter. Had they been growing since the beginning of creation? Or were they made that way?

It was a mystery to me how the animals communicated. There were birds singing "Amazing Grace."

I knew every language, along with a heavenly language, and I could speak to anyone with perfect understanding. How could this be?

There were people there who had not died yet. I have heard others say that about heaven. I saw them. And I wondered about this mystery.

Continents, oceans, transparent buildings full of people, kitchens without cooking, factories without power lines, angels with supernatural strength. The mysteries went on and on and kept growing. I wanted to know but was not allowed to know. I knew there was something, but what it was, I didn't know. I asked and asked the angels who were guiding me. Regularly, they told me, "It is not for you to know at this time."

Finally, after many questions about the mysteries I wanted to understand, the angel on my right, who was doing most of the talking, looked at me and sternly said, "The mysteries of God are none of your business."

─────14─────
Prophetic Heaven

"I looked, and there before me was a white horse!
Its rider held a bow, and he was given a crown, and
he rode out as a conqueror bent on conquest."

—Revelation 6:2

There are areas in heaven that are prophetic: they depict things to come. I saw the black tornado of judgment. I saw revival and judgment.

There was a prophetic area that had a landscape that looked like Colorado, with mountains, trees, rocks, and rivers. It had a white-pine pulpit. Two fists came through the sky between the Shekinah glory. The right hand was gold: God's blessing. The left hand was steel: God's judgment.

SEVEN PROPHETIC SIGNS

I saw the Falls of God's Glory, one stream of water falling into vapor on earth. We on earth can rise up to that level. We can rise into the mist of the Falls of God's Glory.

And I saw the Tidal Wave: the last great move of God. It was seven tiers tall. Prophetically, I was told seven signs:

1. The last great move of God will be in out-of-the-way places, day and night.

2. Signs and wonders will increase and be fought against.

3. Laws of physics will be suspended so that the miraculous can flow.

4. Laws of time and space will be made known to men.

5. Knowledge of man will increase and never be based on fleshly things.

6. Sevenfold tidal wave: the last great move of God breaking on the shores of eternity; the greatest part will be poured out in rural areas; "I seek My bride in humble places; I was born in a stable."

7. "Awareness is given My people in days and weeks just before My return."

Mass multitudes will be involved in this revival, which will be through people who give all praise to the Lord. It is coming to root out and destroy the phony. It will keep the faithful, and it will be the introduction to the coming of Christ.

AMPHITHEATERS OF PROMISES

I saw Abraham's amphitheater. It was like a football arena, only hundreds of times larger. There was a cloud in the "playing field" area. In the cloud, I could see all the promises that have come to pass for and because of Abraham. The promises were for the entire world, not just for the Jews. (See Acts 2:38–39.)

There were what looked like two to three million seats with names on them. People had specific promises—promises related to David's throne and the lineage of kings.

Each of the patriarchs had an amphitheater. The angels helped people to remember the promises.

On the way to the Throne, I saw the Amphitheater of David. I didn't go into his building, but I knew about it when I went by. Somehow, I sensed in my spirit, I knew—in heaven, you just know things—that was where David and his descendants went to see their promises coming to pass. But everyone is welcome.

The prayers are precious cargo and are treated as such. No prayer goes unanswered.

I saw a building in the shape of a castle like a cornucopia, or a horn of plenty. It was a Prayer Center. Angels were traveling in and out of the archway at the "speed of light." To go through the archway was to go into the presence of God. The angels were carrying golden censers that carried prayers. They held them by the bowls of the censers. The prayers are precious cargo and are treated as such. No prayer goes unanswered—even wrong prayer. The prayers are brought before the face of God.

Instantly, the angels go back for more.

Fields of Supernatural Supply

I was taken to an area where I looked down upon what looked like millions and millions of acres under cultivation. There are huge fields of grain in heaven that are constantly moving in the breeze. They are a supernatural supply for others of various kinds. There is a heavenly harvest that is prophetic.

At one time in my grandfather's life, he had some land that he had set aside to pay tithes. When he didn't have cash, he used the income from the crops grown on that land to support his church. A drought came: corn wouldn't grow;

beans wouldn't grow. So, he planted wheat in this land because he determined that wheat would grow in pretty dry circumstances. That year of drought, the "tithe" land produced stalks of wheat that were seven feet tall. The people in the area saw and could not explain what had happened except that it was the hand of God. Some said it was a species of wheat they had never seen before. The harvest from that field, by itself, filled the local grain elevator. That is the wheat I saw in heaven.

I saw what seemed like thousands and thousands of trees filled with fruit. Multitudes of people were coming and picking fruit and taking it away in baskets. They took it to their homes in heaven.

There is also a bank in heaven—*our* bank. This is how it works: Every time you give anything, it is recorded in heaven. Angels go to a doorway with a slip. They receive golden coins and bring them to earth. The coins are c hanged to what we need on earth. These are supernatural finances.

There is a heavenly bank through which we supernaturally receive what we need on earth.

Horses in Heaven

The book of Revelation tells us that the Lord will return riding a white horse. (See Revelation 6:2; Revelation 19:11–16.) I have often wondered about that. What would a white horse from heaven actually look like?

I was taken to an area where there were supernatural, horselike creatures. Some of them had wings. Some had abilities that we don't have on earth. They could walk on the air if they needed to.

I saw thousands of chariots and beautiful horses to pull them. All the horses I saw were entirely white. They had red hoofs: fiery, crimson-red hoofs. And huge nostrils. They were about ten to fifteen times bigger than the biggest horses I have ever seen on earth, and they were all muscle, no fat. There was no horse byproduct to clean up, and I don't think they ever ate. They were there for a specific purpose. Some of it had to do with the rapture of the church. The prophet Elijah was taken up to heaven in a fiery chariot. (See 2 Kings 2:9–11.) And I can tell you there was a chariot there that was the Lord's. It was bigger and nicer than the rest, and it was pulled by the most awesome steed.

There were other supernatural animals, also. I saw a beast that had the body of a giant bull, the neck of a camel, and the head of a horse. An angel was sitting on it. I was not told its purpose.

——15——
Classes of Angels

"O LORD Almighty, God of Israel, enthroned
between the cherubim, you alone are God over
all the kingdoms of the earth. You have
made heaven and earth."

—Isaiah 37:16

There are governments in heaven, even though it is an absolute Theocracy. God rules over all from His throne, but He also gives various responsibilities to people and angels, according to His purposes.

Although all believers in heaven are spiritually equal, they have different functions, and certain people may be responsible for overseeing groups of people of various sizes, depending on what God has given them to do. Yet everything is done as a labor of love—never with a sense of superiority over others. This is the government that exists among the saints of heaven.

Angels in heaven also have different ranks and duties. For example, the Bible talks about the *"captain of the host of the LORD"* (Joshua 5:14 KJV) and *"Michael, one of the chief princes"* (Daniel 10:13). I saw at least seventy classes of angels in heaven. They follow their orders to the letter.

I first became aware of just how many classes of angels there were when I was walking on the golden pathway and smelled the fragrance that renewed my strength. I noticed more and more angels of every description and, I believe, of every rank. They were busy with the people, and they were beautiful and were everywhere. Some were in groups; others were by themselves. All were busy doing the business of heaven. As they performed their business, they would stop every few feet and bow their heads, giving silent praise and worship to God.

> *God's angels are beautiful and are everywhere. They are occupied doing the business of heaven.*

But I noticed something, as I mentioned earlier: in heaven, there is no such thing as tomorrow and no such thing as yesterday. It was and is always right now.

I asked one of the angels how time is measured in heaven. He looked at me with a puzzled expression on his face. He said, "You mean time as you know it?"

"Yes."

He continued, "Time here is not measured in such trivial things as years, but in ages where the glory of God rolls on forever."

That settled that subject in a big hurry.

The angels took on a new meaning to me. The classes of angels looked like they were family members. Some wore shirts with drawstrings. Some wore pants. Some had shoes. Their hair was never longer than their ears. None had a shaved head, but some had beards. They looked like they were about thirty in human years.

I saw some angels who looked twelve to fifteen feet tall and were as wide as four or five of the biggest linebackers on any NFL team. Some had swords, and some did not. But they were all huge. I was told that they were warfaring an-gels on their way to do battle. I stopped, bowed my head, and backed up a bit. But the angels with me and the voice behind me with a gentle touch—again, I believe this was Jesus—said, "You have nothing to fear. They are about the Father's business."

RECORD-KEEPING ANGELS

Then I noticed other groups of angels. Some were tall and slender. One of them I had seen before in several vi-sions I have had in my life. He was there. It was the first time I had noticed him. He was standing off to the side watching everything I did and listening to everything I said. And he had a large book. He was writing in it with a quill that must have been six feet long—it was huge and golden. The book he was writing in was made out of some type of golden-looking material and might have weighed several hundred pounds on earth. But he held it in his left hand, writing with his right. It was as if it weighed nothing to him.

I know I had seen him before. Now, the Word tells us that God keeps a record of every thought and every deed and ev-ery action that we do on earth. (See, for example, Hebrews 4:13.) I wondered at this when I saw this angel writing. Now I understand that everyone has an angel or angels to record everything that he or she says or does—and God knows it.

In the book of Revelation, we find that the "books are opened."

And I saw the dead, great and small, standing be-fore the throne, and books were opened. Another book was opened, which is the book of life. The dead were

judged according to what they had done as recorded
in the books.   (Revelation 20:12)

THE ARMIES OF GOD: WARFARING ANGELS

I saw what I call the Armies of God. I was taken to a very large area that wasn't in the city. I don't know where it was, and I don't know what part of heaven it was in, but I was taken there in an instant. I was in the air, and I looked down on possibly hundreds of thousands of angels lined up in ranks and in units. They looked just like soldiers getting ready to go on parade.

I knew—I understood supernaturally—that they were standing right where they had been positioned by God when He first created them for His purposes. They were God's warfaring angels, and they would leave heaven and come down to fight battles for us. Then, they would go back to heaven and stand in formation until they were needed again. Some of them had swords that looked fifteen feet long and were on fire. The swords looked like they were made of flaming material. These angels were not what you would call tall and slender, such as I had seen in some parts of heaven. Nor were they friendly looking or kindly looking, like other angels I saw in heaven and still see today.

> *God's warfaring angels come down to earth to fight battles for us.*

I have seen these warfaring angels before. God has shown them to me here on earth, but not as often as other types of angels. These were fearsome angels dressed in battle garb. They didn't have helmets, but they had huge shields, flaming swords, and spears that were about thirty feet long. They must have stood twenty feet tall and weighed the better part of a ton, according to earthly measurement. They were huge, muscular angels. They looked like a Mr. America—but considerably larger!

Some of them had short-sleeved garments, while others had long-sleeved garments. Some were dressed in a type of a tunic and pants outfit with drawstrings around the neck. Others were clothed with just light.

They had supernatural weapons that I do not know how to explain. I knew that some of them could speak words and cause whole nations to crumble and fall into the sea. They were armed, some with words, some with swords, some with spears that had special purposes, and all with the power of God. And they knew their jobs—their highly specialized jobs. Nobody had to tell them *how* to do them. God just told them *where* to do them.

All the angels whom I saw were very specialized, and each one had an intended purpose. Some of them were clothed with the power to move the earth, and others were clothed with the power to bring judgment, but they all had power to defend and to keep God's children.

I looked down and said, "Look at those mighty angels."

The angels standing with me stood at attention and said, "Behold the warfaring angels of God. They are mighty to the pulling down of the strongholds of the evil one." (See 2 Corinthians 10:4 KJV.)

I noticed that all their hands were clothed with power, and I asked, "Why are their hands aflame?" I was told that they are ready at any moment to come and do battle against the powers of the devil that assail us. They are ready at any moment to come and be on assignment to deliver from the power of the devil. The power of God is in their hands to accomplish all that He wants them to do.

They were mighty, and they were lined up rank and file: hundreds upon hundreds of them. I looked at them and knew that they are released to fight for us the minute we mention the name of Jesus.

I saw thousands of them coming and going from their rank and file in the place where they stood to come and do battle on earth. They would come out of the ranks almost at the speed of light and disappear. I knew that they were going to earth to help someone.

Oh, the power of God that is there and available for us! If we only knew how much the angels have to do with our victory here and how God wants us to have victory all of the time!

WISDOM-GIVING ANGELS

I saw that there were multitudes and multitudes of angels in another place who were given to us for wisdom. They would go to the Library of God's Knowledge and get wisdom and bring it to us. Or, they would go with a special instruction to bring it and cause it to happen on earth.

There are multitudes of angels whose purpose is to bring God's wisdom to us on earth.

I also saw that the Holy Spirit was in charge of it all—He leads, He guides, He directs, and He gives instructions to the angels. The angels do not act on their own, but only under the auspices of the Lord Jesus and the power of the Holy Spirit. Only the name of Jesus can loose the angels for us. When we mention the name of Jesus in our prayers, the

Holy Spirit immediately begins to direct the action and the angels of God to come into play for us.

PROTECTING ANGELS

I saw that each person who is born again doesn't have only one or two angels. There are literally legions of angels who are at the disposal of the Holy Spirit on our behalf. I saw angels who were in charge of the weather, and I saw angels who were in charge of protection.

Many times in my life, God has sent angels to me. One time, while we were driving, I was given a vision of angels mounted on beautiful, white horses, and they were traveling along with us beside our automobile. I could see them just like I saw them in heaven. And I could hear them. We had been praying for protection, and my wife was driving. Suddenly, my spiritual eyes and ears were opened, and I heard one of the angels say to me, "I can go faster than you can." I thought that was strange, and I told my wife. She said she had been thinking, *I wonder what would happen if I put my foot on it*. Angels were listening. It is important that we, as the children of God, keep our thinking right, keep our words right, and allow God to go into action for us.

ANGELS FOR ALL OF GOD'S PURPOSES

I saw what appeared to be millions and millions of angels for the many purposes that God has intended in heaven. But I was not allowed to see all of them. The angels would not speak to me unless it was the perfect will of God for them to do so. They are totally obedient to God.

Anytime Jesus was near, the angels would stand at attention and look at Him with the greatest adoration. They would fall at His feet if He wanted to speak to them. They were actually there to serve us as children of God and to serve God in whatever capacity He desired. They were energized to do that. They were empowered to do anything that He wanted them to do.

Entertaining Angels Unaware

I somehow knew that there were other areas of heaven where I could not go and that there were other classes of angels I was not allowed to see—different types. I was not allowed to know anything about them. But I do know that some of the angels took the form of people and came to earth. Scripture tells us that we may have shown hospitality to angels without realizing it:

> *Be not forgetful to entertain strangers: for thereby some have entertained angels unawares.*
>
> (Hebrews 13:2 KJV)

Certainly, we all have heard stories of people believing they have encountered angels in such a way. I saw that the angels who took the form of people actually came from heaven to do the purpose that God intended.

——16——
Castle of Dreams

*"Delight yourself in the LORD and he will give
you the desires of your heart."*

—Psalm 37:4

My angel companion to my right said, "I have brought you here to observe this portion of heaven." He said no more, and he wasn't going to. The angel on the left, who usually said very little, bowed his head in deep respect and adoration and began to praise the Lord. I fell silent. I just wanted to do the same thing.

Immediately in front of me was the largest castle I could ever imagine. It was suspended in the air many thousands of feet above ground, and there were mountains all around. It was the most beautiful castle imaginable, and it was completely crystal clear.

The castle seemed to extend for miles in all directions. From the outside, you could not see anyone inside, even though you could see right through it. Yet, when I went through the massive gates, I saw that it was filled with what looked like thousands of people. These "people" seemed to be heavenly beings who took care of the business of the castle. There were also great rooms of books, with thousands of angels tending them.

Three Diadem trees grew in the courtyard. They were smaller than the first one I had seen but just as splendid. The angel said, "Remember this," and, suddenly, we were gone.

At the time, I didn't understand the meaning of the castle. Later, however, the Lord took me aside and shared it with me. "Remember the crystal castle in the sky?" He asked. "That is the place where the hopes and the dreams of My people are kept and fulfilled." God keeps the hopes and dreams that He wants to fulfill in our lives.

> *The castle of dreams is where the hopes and dreams of God's people are kept and fulfilled.*

While I was there, I knew the name of the castle, but it was wiped from my mind. All I know is that there is a place where the hopes and dreams that God gives us are stored for us. The angels became very respectful in the presence of the hopes and dreams God has for us. They bowed low.

"Now, it is time for your appointment before the Throne." They bowed low at the very thought. Then, they simultaneously stood tall, erect, and at attention. The angel spoke to me, "Your time has come to go to the Throne."

17

The Throne of God

"Salvation belongs to our God, who sits
on the throne, and to the Lamb."

—Revelation 7:10

Instantly, we were at the Throne of God. From the moment I got there, I understood that everything in heaven flowed into and out of the Throne. It pulsed like a dynamo. Everything was drawn to the Throne. Everything cycled around the Throne of God.

The Throne Building was huge—beyond my ability to understand. It was the biggest building in heaven. It looked several hundred miles wide and at least fifty miles tall, and it had a domed roof. There were living statues with flames coming out of them. And there were columns that looked as if they were thirty to thirty-five feet across.

STEPS TO THE THRONE

Thousands of steps led up to the Throne. I don't know the exact number, but I do know that each step was significant and prophetic.

As we began to go up the stairway, I saw hundreds of thousands or perhaps millions of people going into and coming out from the Throne. They were worshipping and praising God. One person said, "He is all I thought He was and much more." I heard someone else say, "I just want to go back so bad." He was answered with, "When God's time is right, you will be back here."

A thousand steps up—every step had a purpose.

Something was done to me to be able to withstand the presence of God. The closer I got, the more magnificent everything became. Proximity causes the tangible things in heaven to become more and more splendid.

> *The closer I got to the Throne, the more magnificent everything became.*

The entry area, or gateway, had columns. The number of the columns was also prophetic. Like everything else, they were huge, and I have no idea how many there were. There were additional columns that were tremendously tall and looked like they were a thousand feet across. They were in the doorway leading into the Throne.

Suddenly, we were through the columns. There were millions multiplied by millions of people prostrate on their faces toward the Throne of God, which somehow faced every direction at the same time. The Throne looked like it was twenty-five miles tall. From any part of heaven, you can see the Throne of God.

PROSTRATE BEFORE GOD

The Throne was still quite a far way off in the distance, but even at this distance, the angels were in awe and were prostrating themselves. I found myself on my face before God. All I wanted to do was worship and praise Him.

The Throne was made out of some heavenly material. It was crystal clear, yet it consisted of what appeared to be gold and ivory and silver and precious gems and jewels—all sparkling. It gave off what looked like light rays, which came out of the material it was made of. Great waves of glory swept through it—liquid fire going through the building material. The building itself gave off rays of glory.

Something had happened to my eyes, and I was able to look at the things of God, or else they would have been too brilliant for my natural eyes.

God on the Throne

From this distance, I could tell that there was a Being on the Throne. But He was covered with a cloud of glory that radiated from Him: an all-consuming, enfolding fire that was the glory of God Himself. He dwelt in a fire of glory.

The fire must have been the same thing Moses saw in the burning bush. Whatever it was, it surrounded the Being on the Throne. I could tell that there was a Throne, and I could tell that there was a Being in the fire, and I could tell that He was looking at me.

I felt like a grain of sand on the seashore, and I wanted to crawl under other people. I was actually in the presence of the almighty God.

Such reverential fear fell upon me—not a dread, but a reverential fear of actually being in the presence of the almighty God. Unbelievable. That reverential fear fell on everybody as they got closer and closer to the Throne.

I could not stand.

Thousands upon thousands of people were going in and out. There were millions of people around the Throne worshipping God. Some were standing. I'm not sure why. Perhaps they had already been lying down or God had instructed them to stand. But most were lying on their faces before God, thanking Him for what He had done for them.

None of us stands before God on our own merits but only through the righteousness of Christ applied to us: *"For Christ died for sins once for all, the righteous for the unrighteous, to bring you to God"* (1 Peter 3:18). *"Christ Jesus...has become for us wisdom from God—that is, our righteousness, holiness and redemption"* (1 Corinthians 1:30).

Inside the Throne Room were seven big pillars. And then there were nine pillars of a substance near to God. I believe they are the gifts of the Spirit.

There was an inner court surrounded by pillars. There was also a pavement area with millions of people lying prostrate—some on their backs—all facing the Throne. The pavement was like the pavement Jesus had stood on, with what seemed like a hundred thousand acres of inlaid jewels.

The Throne had a foundation, but I was not allowed to know more.

COALS FROM THE ALTAR OF GOD

As I got closer to the Throne, I noticed an area with a railing. Actually, there were three levels of railings. Humans are not allowed beyond them. The railings are made of gold and some other kind of material that radiates the glory of God and may be the same as the glory of God. Angels stood at the railings.

Around the area were stones that were on fire; living stones shaped like a potato gave off blue and amber Shekinah glory. They were from the altar of God and roughly two feet in diameter. They looked like they were coals from the altar of God, and on each one of them was a name. My name was on one of these coals before the altar of God. Again, I was instantly on my face before Him. All I wanted to do for all eternity was give glory, honor, and praise to God. The feeling was multiplied millions of times over, stronger and stronger, but it is the same feeling that I have now, on earth, when I am in deep prayer and seeking God: I don't want to come out.

THE GLORY OF GOD

While I was in the glory cloud, I was not allowed to look very far. When I would try to lift my head, something would push it back down. It was not as if I could see God clearly—I couldn't—but I could tell there was a Being on the Throne.

Again, I never saw God plainly. I was not allowed to see Him except for one of His feet. His foot seemed the size of the United States, and His toe looked the size of Tennessee. I don't understand how this could be, but this was my impression. These are just my words in an attempt to describe the indescribable.

The Word declares, *"This is what the LORD says: 'Heaven is my throne, and the earth is my footstool'"* (Isaiah 66:1). I understand now how the world could be His footstool.

The glory He was clothed with radiated from Him, sounding like millions upon millions of dynamos of surging current.

Whoosh.

Whoosh.

There was just surge upon surge of power. Supernaturally, I knew that these surges of power were answers to someone's prayer. God answers prayer from His glory.

Then, there was a raised area beyond this magnificence. There were beings on the throne, and flames went in and out. Around the Throne were winged creatures that flew around and around, saying, "Holy, holy, Lord God Almighty." I actually saw them doing just that, but I can't describe them. I know that every time they went around the Throne, they saw a different aspect of God. He was totally revealed to them. (See Isaiah 6:1–3; Revelation 4:6–8.)

Four rivers flowed from the Throne. They came out of the glory cloud and washed over the coals from the altar of God but did not extinguish them—there was no hissing sound; they could not be put out. The rivers came out as one from the Throne, flowed across the pavement, and then continued on to the areas prepared for them as they became four distinct flowings of water. The small streams looked about half a mile wide. They flowed through heaven and appeared bottomless. One of the rivers was the flow of the mercy and grace of God.

All this time, I saw memorials to the glory of God for what is done. I saw Jesus talking to others, and yet He always seemed to be behind me. There was what looked like a band shell at the Throne of God. Jesus was there. He looked at me, and I just had no words. I still cannot describe how I felt as He looked at me. It seemed important to Him that I noticed Him. Everything in heaven notices Him, but, for some reason, He wanted me to remember this. I looked on Him, and He smiled.

Whew!

There is a Scripture that says not to fear those who can destroy the body, but to fear Him who can destroy the body and soul in hell. That is God alone. He has the power of eternity.

And fear not them which kill the body, but are not able to kill the soul: but rather fear him which is able to

destroy both soul and body in hell.
(Matthew 10:28 KJV)

In front of the Throne, I saw a laver, or basin, filled with the blood of Jesus.

Liquid plasma, waves of glory flowed out from the Throne. The hopes and desires of everyone who has ever lived flowed into the Throne. And out of the Throne flowed God's love and the answers to our prayers. All were there.

> *Our hopes and desires flowed into the Throne, and God's love and the answers to our prayers flowed out of the Throne.*

I noticed that the people who were in heaven did not necessarily get to see God right away. Sometimes, they had to wait for a long time. I think they have to be there for a while to be able to withstand being in His presence. There is something about eating that fruit and smelling those beautiful leaves as you come into the garden that helps you to withstand the very presence of God—to keep you from just melting.

There were waves of liquid love coming out of God. The fragrance would choke you on earth. But the aroma of God's presence is beautiful beyond belief. Sometimes, in revival services here, I have noticed a heavenly fragrance that has been released. We have smelled it many times, but not at the intensity that it was in a place called heaven.

Out of the glory of God, I saw a puff of smoke that went by me like a big plane—millions of dynamos. This was my anointing being sent.

I watched the angels who brought prayers. They were given the substance of God sent with an answer. Everything—all answers—are designed out of His glory.

When it is time to leave the Throne, you migrate back to what you are to do. Every person has a God-designed purpose.

Unbelievable Peace and Tranquility

I was before the Throne for what I thought was a long time, but, suddenly, I was no longer there. I'd been carried from the Throne because I could not walk. I was glowing with light and could not speak, either. But I was not the only one in this state. All who had come from the Throne were in about the same condition, and all were giving God the glory.

Unbelievable peace and tranquility.

Indescribable.

Then, the angel told me, "You have an appointment with the Lord."

Instantly, I was in a parklike setting, traveling at the speed of thought toward something like a gazebo.

—— 18 ——
An Audience with the Master

*"The one who is in you is greater than
the one who is in the world."*

—1 John 4:4

I heard a voice saying, "You are destined to an audience with the Master."

Jesus stood on a platform in a gazebo. He appeared to weigh about 180–190 pounds in earthly terms, and He had a reddish-brown beard. He had scars on His face and neck—open wounds that were not healed. His feet were also scarred. He wore a seamless robe of light and was engulfed in a glory cloud of light.

There were seats around the gazebo. The Lord turned, and His attention was on something else. When He turned, I fell flat on my face. The power of God just knocked me right down.

Somehow, He stood me on my feet. He must have touched me. The angels were also on their faces. He told them something, but I don't remember it.

"Sit. I have somewhat to say to you," He said. There was a golden chair; again, it was shaped like wrought iron.

Jesus told me, "When you were a child, I came to you."

When I was seven years old, I saw Jesus come down on a golden stairway. When I was four years old, I was caught away to heaven while I was at my grandfather's house. My grandfather was quite a gentleman and a Bible reader. He was a protégé of evangelist Billy Sunday; they were great friends. That day, I had gone outside to catch grasshoppers, before my grandfather and I were to go fishing, because he had told me, "It's my time to pray." He sat praying and watching me from the dining room window. I remember reaching down to pick up a grasshopper, and the next thing I knew, I was in heaven standing before the throne of God. I'll never forget it—there were royal purple tapestries everywhere and big columns. Jesus was sitting on the throne, and He looked down at me and smiled. He said, "Never drink, never smoke, never sin—there's work for you to do later on." Then, I re-

> **Jesus was sitting on the throne, and He looked down at me and smiled.**

member jumping, and I don't know how long I was frozen in that posture, but when I looked up to the window again, I saw that Grandpa had a big grin on his face because he knew what had happened. He had probably prayed for it and then prayed it through. I told him, and he was very excited about it.

Now, in my heavenly audience with the Master, Jesus said to me, "I have called you as a prophet to the nations. In many ways, you have succeeded. In many ways, the evil one hindered and overcame you. But fear not; I have overcome him. I was there when you were born. I was there when you were four and the evil one tried to destroy you."

As a young child, I had contracted measles, scarlet fever, and other sicknesses. The doctor had given up on me. My mother was rocking me while my dad was in the field plowing. Suddenly, the house filled with smoke as if it was on fire, but there was no smell of fire. My mother cried out, "God, if

You spare this boy...." Out of the cloud came two hands that healed me.

"Son, I'm going to take you to the other place," Jesus now said. "I want to do more through you. Richard, I need your help. You were never designed to be more than what you are. This is heaven, where I want My people to come."

Thousands of people were listening to what He was saying to me. He told me about people who were currently in my life and those who would later come into my life. He told me some very personal and private things about my life. He told me some of the heartaches and troubles that I would have— the things that I would go through:

"One is and will not be, and one is next to come."

"Beware, the evil one would send you to wrong people."

Jesus said that the great revivals were about to spring out in His church. He was going to cause great revivals to come in small places, and I would be on earth to see them. He also talked to me of many other things.

> *Jesus said that the great revivals were about to spring out in His church.*

Holding His hands out flat, He gestured and said, "All is taken and brought together."

—19—
The Other Place

"Do not be afraid of those who kill the body but cannot kill the soul. Rather, be afraid of the One who can destroy both soul and body in hell."

—Matthew 10:28

Come. My Father wills you to see the other place," Jesus said. Immediately, I felt dread and did not want to go. Jesus looked at me and said, "There is no disobedience in heaven," and I was ready to go. I knew that because I was with Jesus, I would be perfectly safe.

> *I knew that because I was with Jesus, I would be perfectly safe.*

Jesus picked me up and carried me like a baby. There was no give to His body; it felt as hard as steel. He has all-powerful arms; He is the strongest Being in the universe.

Instantly, we descended into a gray, nasty stench, like a rotting carcass. I buried my face in His robe.

"You will not want to see," He said, and I was scared. I had both of my arms wrapped around one of Jesus' arms. We descended to a flat area, and I was at the gates of total destruction.

I quickly realized that hell is the exact opposite of everything that heaven is. The gates were as big as the gates in heaven, but these were made of a black material. I remember stairs. And there were hideous, grotesque beings as tall as the angels who guarded the gates of heaven. Some cartoon figures of demons approach how hideous these creatures were. When they saw the Master, they screamed in horror.

There were also flames of punishment. I felt the doom and despair there. I heard people crying out. It seems that demons take people and torture them to the same level of pain the demons themselves are in—or worse. People were naked. There was no one there who was not old enough to know what sin was. There were no babies.

Jesus urged me to tell people what I saw. "I want you to tell others of this place and warn them that unless they are washed in My blood, unless they are born again, this is where they will spend eternity."

There were demons all around, screaming, screaming, screaming at the very presence of Jesus. They could not stand to be in His presence. As soon as they saw Him, they screamed and ran in terror.

There were people begging and pleading with Jesus to get them out of there, but He would not hear them because their judgment was fixed. (See Hebrews 9:27.)

I cannot describe everything I saw because it makes me violently ill. I don't want to remember. But I can tell you that there is absolute horror.

When you die, you have a spiritual body. This spiritual body has the exact properties that your physical body had when you were alive. You are a spirit being, yet all physical senses are present.

I saw people in hell who were no more than walking skeletons with flesh of some kind hanging off of them—rotting off of them. There were maggots, and the smell was unbreathable. People were being raped. Serpents ate and digested parts of people; then, the people were restored and it happened all over again.

I witnessed people being ripped apart by demons. Parts of their bodies were hanging on boulders and rocks, and the demons would take the parts and eat them and pass them through. And then the body was whole again for the process to be repeated.

A young girl had hot coals forced into her mouth as demons mocked, "You really thought you were getting by with something."

There were groups of people in small cages that were on fire. People were put into small, burning cages that were then dipped in a lake of fire. However, their bodies were not consumed. The bodies were never consumed. They were half skeletons/half beings.

Demons poured liquid fire on people. There were what looked like coal pits burning.

People had cancer, with all its pain and suffering—forever.

One man had a rotting arm. It took a hundred years to rot off. Then, it was restored, only to begin rotting off again.

There was another man with part of his head blown off from war. He had to keep looking for the rest of his head.

I saw the lake of fire with people in it, bobbing around. Every torment you can imagine is multiplied a million times.

There are degrees of punishment in hell. The people who are punished the greatest are those who knew the most and didn't do what they should have done. I thought of Hitler, and I thought of God's justice.

There was a hole, and in the bottom of the hole demons were chained. When they saw Jesus, they screamed out, "We're coming to get You!" But Jesus said. "No, you won't."

I pleaded, "Please, I don't want any more."

There were pits of hell that were empty—empty now, but waiting for whole nations.

It was dark, and there were demons and serpents everywhere. The demons inflicted more pain than they were going through themselves.

And they will go out and look upon the dead bodies of those who rebelled against me; their worm will not die, nor will their fire be quenched, and they will be loathsome to all mankind.   (Isaiah 66:24)

Then, I saw the place reserved for the devil and his angels: he will have flaming, slimy fire over his head for a thousand years. The lake of fire had depths that got worse and worse and worse.

"Son, you have fulfilled what God wanted," Jesus said. We ascended to the platform again.

I asked, "Who am I going to tell?"

"Tell others about a place called heaven—and the other place, the place of separation."

He took my face in His hands and tilted it so that I had to look directly into His face. Then, He said, "Don't ever forget how much I love you and what I have done for you. Never forget how much I love those whom you are going back to and the place I have prepared for them and how much I love them."

> *"Tell others about a place called heaven," Jesus said.*

—20—
The Second Throne Experience

*"You alone are the LORD....You give life to everything,
and the multitudes of heaven worship you."*

—Nehemiah 9:6

Iknew that I was not yet going to get to stay in heaven. I
was told very plainly, yet softly and tenderly, that I would
have to go back.

I found myself standing by Jesus' side. He was talking
to some people gathered around Him, and He was telling
them how much He loved them. I could do nothing but stand
speechless. Until you have heard the Master speak and express His love for us, you cannot completely understand why
I was unable to speak. The meaning that we humans give to
love pales in comparison with the purity, the depth, and the
true meaning of what His love is like. We know so little next
to the One who loved so much that He gave His life for all so
that we could someday live with Him in heaven.

Then, Jesus put His arm around my shoulders and hugged
me to Himself, and I wept uncontrollably. I was engulfed in
a torrent, a flood of the greatest love and most absolute acceptance that I have ever known.

AT THE CENTER OF ALL EXISTENCE

Then, instantly, I was at the Throne Room again. I fell
like a dead man. All I knew was that I was at the center of

all existence and that the Creator of all things was there. I was completely bathed in His love.

With all that is within me, I yearn to go back to heaven for eternity. There were scenes there so beyond my understanding that I don't even want to speak of them, for you would not believe them.

There was a fragrance that permeated everything that seemed to be a link between the very presence of God and all of heaven. It was absolutely a rapture of pure wonderment. I was told it was the fragrance of God. I fell before the Lord prostrate when I heard these words.

Everywhere I looked, I saw people completely at peace. Absolute joy and total love are the rule in heaven.

Absolute joy and total love are the rule in heaven.

There were sights and sounds that I can never adequately tell or articulate in any human vocabulary. There were structures and amphitheaters beyond description. You would not be able to comprehend or believe the total scope of what I was allowed to witness for the sake of my generation.

The laws of earth—laws of physics and all the laws of the universe as we know them in our human understanding—did not apply there. Only the will of God in a heavenly sense applied there.

All the time I was allowed to be in heaven, I witnessed wonder upon wonder.

The Lord Jesus was always there at the moment that was perfect for His appearing. I cannot explain it any better, so I will say again, I am just telling you what I was shown.

People would silently look with adoring eyes and whisper, "He is coming." I witnessed an absolute worship of our

Savior that human beings will never be able to enter into in this life. I shall always hold this most dear to my heart, forever.

The Most Beautiful Spot in Heaven

The Throne Room of God was the most beautiful spot in heaven.

During my second visit to the Throne Room, I was taken to an area that I had not noticed during my first visit because I had been so overwhelmed by the presence of God. I was to experience even more this time.

In this area, there were what appeared to be rooms in a high, arched cathedral. They were all along a side wall, across from a living statue of the Lord Jesus. Again, the statue was alive; it moved and it spoke. I have no way of explaining it. I can only tell you what I witnessed in the best way that I know how.

The Covenant of Jehovah

The rooms had arched entrances that led into a large area that was totally private. I saw my name, RICHARD OF THE FAMILY OF SIGMUND, and under it these words:

THE COVENANT OF JEHOVAH, AND THE REDEEMED
OF THE LAMB.

I was shaking and unable to make even a sound. Sometimes, silence is golden.

On a beautiful, pulpit-like structure was a book that looked like a Bible. It was signed across the front with these words: "My covenant will not break. I will not alter the thing that has gone out of My mouth."

I was astonished. I was reminded of the shed blood of the Lord and of the price He paid to redeem me, and again, I wept uncontrollably.

The book opened by itself, and then, suddenly, Jesus was there by my side. He said, "This is My plan for your life, and I will honor it as long as you honor it and live under My Father's demand for your life."

I fell at His feet and cried, "Holy is the Lord my God." I never knew the power of covenant in that realm before, and I will never forget it. It shall stand for eternity.

There were other rooms, also—one for each born-again believer. You see, God has plans for each one of us—eternal plans.

A City of Homes by the Seashore

I didn't want to leave, but, somehow, I knew that I had no choice. Yet I had great joy in knowing that it pleased God to speak so personally to me. I was overjoyed, to say the least. I was then taken to an area near the crystal clear seashore. It was a city of homes that actually floated above the treetops. The buildings were smaller than some of the others I had seen but were magnificent to look at. I was told that some of heaven's citizens desired homes on the seashore, and other places, as well. Then, there were those who wanted to have their homes anywhere that they happened to be. I marveled at the love of God. How He loves to provide our hearts' desires when our

God loves to provide our hearts' desires when our ways please Him!

ways please Him! I saw children, and older people, too, floating down from their homes and walking on. I also saw some people walking on the water. I marveled again at this, and I was told, "With God, all things are possible." (See Matthew 19:26.)

I felt a desire to walk on the water. There is no fear or dread in heaven, or anything like that. There are no negative emotions; they simply do not exist there. Instead, there is a deep desire to please God. There is joy, peace, and love. There is perfect harmony.

I then stepped out on the water. I turned to look back, and there was Jesus, beaming with joy. He was smiling the same type of amused smile people have when they see a wide-eyed child opening presents on Christmas morning. It brought joy to Him, and it reminded me of God's father nature.

I couldn't help but give glory to God.

THE ROSE GARDEN

"Come. You have another appointment with Jesus," the angel said as he bowed his head in complete humility. "Come now. The Master awaits."

I was taken to a beautiful rose garden. The Rose Garden is God's personal place in heaven. His favorite place. There were actually rose bushes that were as large as trees here on earth. They had roses of every type and description. Some were nearly transparent, yet they exploded in a burst of thousands of colors. Most of these colors would be impossible to capture here on earth. I marveled exceedingly.

There, in the center, was a sitting place with garden-type furniture made of solid gold.

But most of all, and best of all, Jesus was there waiting for me. Again, I fell at His feet, but the only sound I could utter was a very weak, "My Lord and Savior." I was weeping with great joy.

Everything in heaven seems to stand still when the Lord Jesus speaks. There were several of the ministering class of angels there. The Lord was giving them instructions. I could not hear, or was not supposed to hear, what was being said.

There were several other people there, also. Somehow, I was able to grasp the significance of the moment. Who was I to be there? I will never know.

I recognized one of the men from my ministering years on earth. I wanted to reach out and embrace him. It was so good to see him.

There were others I knew personally, and some I had only heard about. There were also some who were Bible figures. I was so wobbly kneed, I just stood there and trembled. And then, it seemed as though all of them, in unison with their words, let me know that they would see me again soon, and we would have a reunion that would last a century.

This pleased me very much.

THE MASTER SPEAKS

I was told to sit and just listen. It seemed again as though all of heaven grew silent. I really believe it did.

As the Lord approached, I once again fell at His feet. A hand as strong as steel lifted me up, and I was looking into the Master's face once again. He gave me a loving, all-knowing look of absolute acceptance.

I was trembling with ecstasy and peace. He said, "Sit down," and I sat immediately, still trembling.

Then, Jesus drew back a few steps and began to speak. "For centuries, men have tried to interpret My Word. Some were correct, in as much light as they had. Some were wrong, and some of them were sent by the evil one to lead My

Father's creation astray. From the day that My grace was extended to redeem creation, the evil one has tried to steal it from My hands. But until the day that I will soon return, that which My Father has committed to Me will not be taken from Me. I have worked to make salvation available to all. I was there when the first rays of My glory created the universe. I was there when the planets were made. I did it. I created everything to work perfectly after its own order. For millennia, everything was perfect. I fellowshipped with the first created man in these gardens, until sin became a reality. My Father cast the evil one, and all those who followed him, into outer darkness. They were cast far away from this perfect abode that I have prepared for My bride of faithful believers. The days of creation are numbered. My Father alone knows the number of days. He alone. Soon, I will take the heavenly armies that you have witnessed, along with these elders that are here, and go to get My people. It will be the happiest time of all eternity."

"Soon, I will go to get My people. It will be the happiest time of all eternity."

"You will go back," He said. Immediately, I began to weep at the thought. It hurt so. He reached out and touched my shoulder, and great peace came again.

"Go tell My people what you have seen here. And tell them to get their temples clean and full of My Holy Spirit. Only with My help can they endure to the end."

—— 21 ——
"You Are Going Back"

*"Behold, I am coming soon! My reward is with me,
and I will give to everyone according to what he has
done. I am the Alpha and the Omega, the First and
the Last, the Beginning and the End. Blessed are
those who wash their robes, that they may have
the right to the tree of life and may go
through the gates into the city."*

—Revelation 22:12–14

Jesus said, "You are going back." I sighed, and Jesus rebuked me. "The will of My Father is never grievous. Stand to your feet. You must go back. You will come back to heaven. You will have angelic visits," He said. Then, Jesus hugged me.

Suddenly, my body was full of pain. There was a sheet over my face. I could feel my bones knitting together; I was being healed. I heard a voice say, "He's been dead all these hours."

I could feel my left wrist where the bone had been protruding—I could feel it popping into place and healing up.

"It is about time to embalm him."

I remember sitting up and saying, "I ain't dead yet."

Someone hollered in the hall, "He's alive! That dead man is alive!" I remember a doctor coming in and saying, "I pronounced him dead, and he is dead."

But I was sitting up.

Other doctors and nurses came in, and I began to tell the story of where I had been and what had happened. People were weeping. Doctors said, "This must be a miracle of God."

Since My Time in Heaven...

To this day, nobody knows how the accident with my van happened. There were no other cars around. It looked as if both the front and the back of the van had been hit by Sherman tanks at the same time. The policeman said that it looked like God had clapped His hands, and I'd been in the middle of them.

As you can imagine, my time in heaven changed the nature of my life on earth. All I've ever wanted to do was to win the lost to Jesus, pray for the sick, and help believers become filled with the Holy Spirit. Telling about my experience in heaven has made it easier for me to minister in these ways because people come to my services with a greater sense of expection of what God can do. I've always had large numbers of people attend my meetings, but my testimony seems to have opened things up much more. It has had an impact that is beyond anything that occurred before—and it's been the work of God all the way.

Supernatural Manifestations and Increased Ministry

Since my heavenly experience, I have continued to have visitations of the Lord. God has poured out His Spirit into my life. I have witnessed the blind see, the deaf hear, and the lame walk, and I have literally seen the dead raised.

A man dropped dead across from my driveway. By the time the ambulance arrived, the man hadn't breathed for fifteen minutes, but, after prayer, he came back to life.

In another case, a man was working on building a church in Mexico when an adobe brick fell on his head and crushed his skull. He died instantly. Everyone gathered around him and prayed, and God raised him up. Then, he said, "I was in heaven, and I didn't want to come back!"

So, this happens more often than we think. When I was about fourteen or fifteen years old and was ministering with A. A. Allen, we went to see a young woman in the hospital who'd had kidney disease and had suffered a stroke. She had died in that hospital and been pronounced dead. But A. A. Allen and others prayed for her, even though she had been dead for about an hour. The woman's father, who was an undertaker, came to see about her body, but when he got to the hospital, she was alive again. The very next night, she went to church, and she didn't look like she'd been sick a day in her life. That was a miracle!

There have been other miracles, as well. There was a man in the hospital who had a broken leg, which the doctors couldn't seem to realign so that it could heal. They called my friend Pastor Randy Wallace and me to come and pray. God set that bone before our very eyes, and his leg was healed.

In every service, I see the outpouring of the Holy Spirit and God performing the miraculous. When I tell my story, there are always a great number of people who want to get right with God. If I were in their situation, *I* would, too. I would want to go to a place called heaven!

I also continue to have angelic visitations. Even though I have never again seen the two angels who escorted me through heaven—as far as I know—I have had numerous other angelic visitations. And God is much more rich and much more free to me.

I have a depth of God in my life now that I never knew was possible. It just seems like this type of revelation is more than any man could ever have. This type of experience with God would seem like one out of a hundred or once in a lifetime, but it now happens to me on a daily basis. Every day, I hear the audible voice of God in some manner. Every day, I see the angels of God. And I have seen Jesus on numerous occasions.

> *Every day, I hear the audible voice of God. Every day, I see the angels of God.*

In revival meetings, the angels are visible to me. The cloud of glory is visible to me. The sickness and diseases in people's bodies are visible to me. The demons that afflict them are visible to me. The glory that comes upon them when God heals them is also visible to me.

Fulfillment of Heavenly Prophecy

Over the years, every once in a while, I have met someone whom I was told in heaven that I would meet on earth. One of those people is Paul Hegstrom, whose heavenly home I'd seen under construction on the avenue named "The Way of the Rose," and whose heavenly library contained the books he would write. (See chapter 8.)

I met Paul through pioneer television evangelist Dr. L. D. Kramer, who is a friend of mine. L. D. mentioned Paul's name to me, and I said, "I know that name." Then, I told him what had happened to me and how I had seen the names of Paul and his wife, Judy, on their home under construction in heaven. Since L. D. Kramer was well-known, he got in touch with Paul on my behalf, and he came down to see me in Texas.

However, I was scared to meet him at first; I didn't know how he would react to what I would tell him. So, I made an excuse that I had to be away from the house. Yet I knew I needed to tell people about my experience, and here God was bringing things to pass, just as He'd said.

Later, when Paul and I met, we became instant friends, and we remain very good friends today. I told him the names of the books I'd seen in his heavenly library, and he said, "We're just now writing those books!"

Another person I had been told I would meet was Sid Roth. I'd seen many things about Sid in heaven. I met him when he called me one day out of the clear blue and wanted to know if I would be on his radio and TV programs. At the time, I was just getting over kidney failure and a stroke, and I wasn't able to get around yet. So, we did a phone interview for his radio program, and we've been friends ever since. Sid said that when I told him my testimony, the presence of God just about knocked him out of his chair. It's been very powerful.

Individuals Touched by God

People continue to be touched by God through my ministry and the story of my experience in heaven. Some of these testimonies are included in a section at the back of this book, but I will share one of them here. An army general serving in Iraq got in touch with me and asked me to ship two cases of an earlier edition of this book. A chaplain distributed the books to the soldiers. One day, one of the soldiers brought his book with him out on patrol. He and his fellow soldiers became pinned down and thought they were all going to be killed. So, of course, they became very religious. They didn't have a Bible, so the soldier started reading out of my book.

The soldiers were trapped behind a wall with the opposing forces closing in. All of a sudden, there was a big thump, like a hand grenade going off, but it seemed to come from the enemy's location. The soldiers peeked over the wall and saw thirty or so enemy combatants running frantically to get away. Immediately, they got out of there.

The next day, they caught some of these combatants and asked them what had happened—why had they run away? They didn't answer at first, but, finally, one of them said, "Well, it's those giants in the sky." Then, several of them related seeing these huge men standing in the sky holding big, long swords. I believe they were angels. One of the angels took his sword and hit the ground right in front of the militants, and that is when they fled. Something sharp had cut that brick wall in two. Bullets won't do that. God had revealed the power of His presence and protection to those pinned-down soldiers who were reading of heaven.

ARE YOU READY FOR ETERNITY?

God has truly poured out upon me a prophetic ministry of signs, wonders, and miracles. I am to tell the story that Jesus is coming soon. Before He sent me back to earth, Jesus told me that I would return, and that when I did, I was to tell His people to get ready—these were the words of the Lord.

Jesus is coming back so that we might go with Him to a place called heaven.

He said, "Prepare yourselves and get ready because I am coming back soon, at a time when people don't think. I am coming back. I am coming back." (See Matthew 24:44; Luke 12:40.) He is coming back for His sons and His daughters; He is coming back for those who serve Him; He is coming back for all of us so that we might go with Him to a place called heaven.

Are you ready? Are you *really* ready? If you aren't, you can be. Turn away from your sins, believe that Jesus Christ died as your Substitute, and confess Him as your Savior and Lord.

If you confess with your mouth, "Jesus is Lord," and believe in your heart that God raised him from the dead, you will be saved. For it is with your heart that you believe and are justified, and it is with your mouth that you confess and are saved. (Romans 10:9–10)

Jesus went into Galilee, proclaiming the good news of God. "The time has come," he said. "The kingdom of God is near. Repent and believe the good news!" (Mark 1:14–15)

Now is the time of God's favor, now is the day of salvation. (2 Corinthians 6:2)

Epilogue:
Where Heaven and Earth Meet

*"Since, then, you have been raised with Christ,
set your hearts on things above, where Christ is seated
at the right hand of God. Set your minds on things
above, not on earthly things. For you died,
and your life is now hidden with Christ in God. When
Christ, who is your life, appears, then you
also will appear with him in glory."*

—Colossians 3:1–4

Multitudes of people who have heard or read my testimony have asked me about the balconies of heaven and how much their loved ones are able to know about those who remain here.

"Caught Up" into the Atmosphere of Heaven

Heaven and earth are more "connected" than most people know—and in ways that are beyond our comprehension. The very nature of heaven is a complete involvement in the plans of God for eternity. Everything has an eternal purpose.

When the spiritual atmosphere and praise and worship are flowing together in perfect harmony, we are dwelling near the Throne of God.

Heaven and earth are joined at times when the spiritual atmosphere and praise and worship are flowing together in perfect harmony. When this happens, we are "caught up" into the atmosphere of heaven itself. No sin, sickness, or disease can dwell there. You are dwelling near the Throne of God.

To access this life-giving flow, we must be in total abandonment to God in adoration, worship, and praise. Only then are we able to be in complete union in this aspect of God's provision for the eternal human spirit. With the help of the Holy Spirit, we all may dwell there.

EVENTS ON EARTH AND IN HEAVEN

In addition, when great movements of the Holy Spirit are happening here in the earthly church, there are corresponding events of praise and worship in heaven. While I was there, I was shown a group of people who had attended a church together on earth. In heaven, they were reunited and attended many heavenly "functions" together. On this day, they were all sitting in the balconies of heaven joining in praise and worship with members of their church on earth. When it was time, everyone would say "Amen" in perfect harmony. Sometimes, the angels of God would join in, as well.

People were told when and where the next "event" on earth would take place. I was told that during Billy Graham's crusades, there were millions of people participating in his services in heaven itself. In addition, legions of angels were dispatched to convict people of sin. This is what happens when we pray and seek God. Heaven gets involved. There are literally tens of thousands of angels who are dispatched to confirm God's Word.

GOD'S KINGDOM ON EARTH

Jesus taught us to pray that God's kingdom would come to earth and that His will would be done on earth as it is in heaven. (See Matthew 6:10.) We need to pursue the nature of God's kingdom, embracing God's character and His purposes for the earth. *"The kingdom of God is...righteousness, peace and joy in the Holy Spirit"* (Romans 14:17). It is imperative that we all live godly, holy lives in the fear and admonition of God. When we do, we may enter into the fullness of Christ.

> *So that the body of Christ may be built up until we all reach unity in the faith and in the knowledge of the Son of God and become mature, attaining to the whole measure of the fullness of Christ.*
>
> (Ephesians 4:12–13)

> *For in Christ all the fullness of the Deity lives in bodily form, and you have been given fullness in Christ, who is the head over every power and authority.*
>
> (Colossians 2:9–10)

NINE STEPS TO THE FULLNESS OF CHRIST

How do we enter into the fullness of Christ? By applying the nature of Christ to our lives.

There are nine steps to the fullness of Christ. They are contained in Galatians 5:22–23. The nature of Christ is revealed there:

> *But the fruit of the Spirit is love, joy, peace, patience, kindness, goodness, faithfulness, gentleness and self-control. Against such things there is no law.*

During a time of intense seeking of God, a friend of mine was driving through the mountains of Arizona. He often passed a particular mountain, and, when he did, he always had the urge to climb it. When he drove past it, he would say, "Someday, I am going to climb this mountain and see what 'this' is all about."

One day, as he was passing the mountain, he decided that would be the day. He climbed until he reached the top. He could see his car way down at the bottom. He was hot and tired, so he stretched out on a rock to rest for a few moments. He must have fallen asleep, because when he awoke, it was well past dark, and the stars were all shining bright.

As he looked up, a bright, shining light shone down out of heaven. Where it struck the ground, an angel stepped out of the light beam. He held up a scroll and said these words: "There are nine steps to the fullness of Christ. You must become perfect in these." On the scroll were the fruit of the Spirit. The first was compassion. You must become perfect in compassion. Then, when compassion has its free course in your life, love will also manifest God's plan in your life. You can't have compassion without extraordinary amounts of God's love. If you want the favor of God, begin to show the compassion of Christ. You must die to self in order to get there.

> *When compassion has its free course in your life, love will also manifest God's plan in your life.*

The medium of exchange in heaven is kindness. This is the gospel itself. It is the law of love:

Love does no harm to its neighbor. Therefore love is the fulfillment of the law.   (Romans 13:10)

The entire law is summed up in a single command: "Love your neighbor as yourself."   (Galatians 5:14)

If you really keep the royal law found in Scripture, "Love your neighbor as yourself," you are doing right.
(James 2:8)

Near the end of my experience in heaven, Jesus said these words:

"My people have lost their compassion."

"I highly desire compassion in My children. In this, they show My Father's love."

"All creation must show love after God's order of being to stand in the favor of God."

I was shown how all heaven follows after the "laws of God's nature." Everyone there was totally engulfed in the perfect nature of God. When He told me this, I began to weep. I knew how much I had failed God in my lifetime. I fell at His feet in worship and praise. He touched me on my left cheek. Then, somehow, I was standing again. I knew I would never be the same again.

Golden Testimonies

Then, I was taken to a beautiful building that stood near the most beautiful trees I have ever seen. They were all different but somehow the same. I can't explain it; I can only tell you what I saw. In the beautiful building, there were what seemed like hundreds of millions of scrolls on golden shelves. All were solid gold of some heavenly kind, with a gold type of material used as a form of paper.

Very reverently, an angel unrolled a scroll. He read from it, saying, "I give God all the glory for my healing. When I surrendered my life to Christ, I was instantly set free from a life of drugs and sin. Now, I am the wife of a pastor here in Milwaukee. Jesus has made it all possible." When I knew who it was, I fell in praise and worship again. All of the testimonies that have ever been given are stored there. Not one is ever lost. Ever.

The angels of God stand in absolute wonderment while a testimony is read. They will never know the saving grace of God. They were created to serve God. And they were created to be His ministering spirits to the heirs of salvation—all born-again believers.

In the next section, I share some of the testimonies I have received. My desire is to encourage you to believe in the Lord Jesus Christ so that you might be present at the marriage supper of the Lamb. (See Revelation 19:6–9.) It is also to inspire your faith so that you might believe God for your miracles of healing.

Testimonies of Salvation, Healing, and Deliverance through the Ministry of Richard Sigmund

INTRODUCTION

I claim no power to heal the sick. The miracles and healing come from God. The Bible gives us many precious promises of God's healing power. (See Mark 16:17–18; John 14:12.) They are God's continuing provision for His people.

In the following testimonies of salvation, healing, and deliverance—many excerpted from letters I have received—names are included where permission was granted. The testimonies have been lightly edited for clarity.

—Richard Sigmund

Dr. Loretta Blasingame and I were staying temporarily in the guest cottage of some friends. Dr. Blasingame suffered a severe fall on the concrete walkway at the cottage and badly injured her head, back, knee, hip, and foot. The pain was unbearable; she was bleeding and had scratches all over her body. She had actually slid on the walkway, and her left hand and arm were gray from the color of the concrete.

Our friends were away at a meeting, so immediately after calling them for help on my cell phone, I used my phone to call Rev. Richard Sigmund to pray Dr. Blasingame's miracle through. The Lord revealed in a vision to Rev. Sigmund that her left foot was broken. As he continued to intercede, he saw in a vision the Lord Jesus placing His hand upon the shattered bones, and he watched as the bones knit together...*perfectly healed*. Rev. Sigmund remained on the cell phone for over an hour, praying over each injured part of her body. The pain ceased and the swelling subsided, and she was able to sit upright on the sidewalk. Amazingly, the blood and scratch marks also disappeared!

> *In a vision, Rev. Sigmund saw Jesus placing His hand upon the shattered bones, and he watched as the bones knit together... perfectly healed.*

Two days later, we decided to have Dr. Blasingame's healing verified by a doctor, and we went to a clinic facility. Many X-rays were taken, and it seemed as if the prognosis was dire, as the X-rays showed that a bone in her left foot was badly fractured and out of place. However, while they were taking more X-rays, we were praying, "Lord, do not let the doctors see anything wrong. Let them see what You have done." After these additional X-rays were taken, the attending physician came in and announced with amazement, "There are no broken bones!"

To God be the glory, and how blessed we were to be able to reach God's chosen servant: Rev. Richard Sigmund!

—Anne W. McAlister
Personal Assistant to Dr. Loretta Blasingame

At one of Richard Sigmund's services, a seventy-six-year-old man came who had lung cancer and had been given six months to live. After Richard prayed for him, this man was able to breathe better and felt a difference in his lungs. He went to the doctor the following week and was 80 percent healed. He then went to his doctor a second time and was 100 percent healed. To God be the glory! The doctor's visits took place within the week after he was prayed for.

Another time, I was asked to go with a friend to visit a young man who was about thirty-two years old and who had stomach cancer and couldn't eat solid food. I could tell that he had lost weight and was a bit thin for his size. I felt impressed to call Richard on my cell phone. So, I asked this young man if he believed in healing and if he'd like prayer for healing, and I told him about Richard and the anointing that is upon his life. He wanted prayer, and Richard prayed for him over the phone. Then Richard asked him to push in on his stomach. He did, and there was no pain! That week, this young man went to his doctor and was found to be 100 percent healed from the stomach cancer! Praise God for His goodness! It's awesome to know that God's anointing can touch people even over the phone!

—Rev. Carol Fraser
Founder/Director, On Eagles' Wings Ministries
Bloomington, MN

I had been a backslider for many years. I was away from God, and I was very heavily into drugs. There was nothing I would not do to get drugs. It was a very dark time in my life. Then, I heard your testimony on the Sid Roth program, *It's Supernatural!* I was listening to a rock concert when the radio station was suddenly changed—and no one had touched it. I heard Sid Roth begin to mention your name, and, immediately, I could not move. I wanted to change the dial, but I could not move.

As I listened to your testimony, I began to feel convicted about my sins and wanted to make things right with God. I wept many bitter tears. When you prayed for those who were listening, I was ready. I am now reunited with my husband and family, and all of us are attending an Assemblies of God Church in Missouri. May God continue to use your heaven testimony.

—Susan B.

I was a member of Pastor Randy Wallace's church in Midlothian, Texas, when my daughter, who was seven months' pregnant, became very ill. The doctor said that her baby had died in her fourth month and that it would have to be surgically removed. You came to church there on a Sunday. I urged my daughter to have prayer so that the surgery would go well the next day. You said, "Come here. God has a miracle for you." As you prayed for her, her stomach began to grow. I couldn't believe what I was seeing. Then, the "dead" baby began to kick and move. The baby is now three years old. We still weep over the miracle God did that Sunday. What a big God we have.

> *You said, "God has a miracle for you." Then, the "dead" baby began to kick and move.*

—Lupe Sanchez
(Editor's Note: This testimony has been affirmed by Pastor Wallace, below.)

A lady in our church was pregnant and came to the Sunday church service after going to the doctor on Friday and learning that the baby she was carrying inside her was dead. There was no heartbeat whatsoever, and the baby wasn't growing. After the service, Richard Sigmund prayed for her, since she was scheduled to have the baby surgically removed the next day. She went back to the doctor and asked him to check the baby again. Not only was there a heartbeat, but the baby had also increased in size substantially. After that, the baby grew incredibly fast, and she was born healthy. I see her from time to time, and there's nothing wrong with her.

Richard and I worked together in a healing revival at Grace Cathedral in Lancaster, Texas. The church had two weeks of evening services, and during that period of time, there were over 270 miracles. Richard would be under the power of God to such an extent that he could not stand up, and I would hold him up. So, I was right there where things were happening and saw miracles firsthand.

There was a lady who had something wrong with her back, and he prayed for her. She was wearing a pantsuit, and I remember looking down at the floor and noticing that her pants suddenly became too short as she was instantly healed. I estimate that she grew three inches.

People who had been diagnosed with all kinds of cancer were healed—several of them had been dying in the last stages of the disease. One man had stomach cancer and hadn't been able to eat anything for a long time. He couldn't hold anything down. I think he was being fed through a tube. Richard prayed for him and then told him, "Go out and eat a steak." The man looked at Richard as if he was insane, but he went out to a restaurant that night and ordered a steak and ate the whole thing! He came back the next night with that testimony, and he grew better and better as time went on. We didn't have a doctor's confirmation, but the man said he was healed. If you cannot eat for a long period of time and then you are able to eat everything that isn't nailed down, you have a pretty good idea that you're healed.

There was a pastor's daughter who was about seventeen or eighteen years old who was brought to the same service in which the man with stomach cancer was healed. From birth, this girl had never been able to hear. Richard prayed for her, and she started screaming. At first, we thought something was wrong, that she might be in pain. But that wasn't the case. She was actually frightened because she was hearing for the first time in her life, and she wasn't used to the sound!

We went to pray for a man who was dying of AIDS. After Richard prayed for him, he no longer had that disease.

In addition, I saw people healed of hernias and heart disease. People also gave testimonies that they were healed of their diabetes during those two weeks of services.

I have seen other miracles through Richard Sigmund's ministry, as well. When I first met Richard, we went to pray for a man in the veterans hospital in Lancaster, Texas, who was dying of AIDS. After Richard prayed for him, he no longer had that disease, according to the doctor's report. This man also had a big knot on his leg, and Richard laid his hands on it and prayed. When he removed his hands, the knot was gone.

These are things I saw personally. I always looked at what was going on objectively to see if it was really a miracle.

When the anointing of the Lord falls on Richard as he's ministering, things happen. God also uses him as a prophet. He once told my wife that when we took a trip, one of her family members would become deathly ill. However, my wife would see a candy cane, which would be a sign for her that everything would be all right. And that's all he told her. Two years later, while we were visiting my wife's family in Kentucky, her sister had a heart attack. They didn't think she was going to make it, and my wife got in the ambulance with her. Yet, as they were driving across the Ohio River, my wife looked down and saw a tugboat coming up the river. Its smokestack was painted just like a candy cane. The moment she saw that, she remembered what Richard had said, and she thanked the Lord. My sister-in-law did not stay in the hospital for even two hours—she recovered that quickly.

I've seen some pretty amazing things through Richard Sigmund's ministry. God definitely uses him in the working of miracles.

—Pastor Randy Wallace
New Hope Christian Center
Midlothian, Texas

I hadn't been in church for such a long time when I attended your meeting in Dallas, Texas. I really didn't want to go, but, to satisfy my friend, I went. I am so very glad I did.

When you prayed for me, my spine was straightened. I grew three inches taller instantly.

No one there knew that I had a severely twisted spine and was in pain all the time. I thought, *I will just have to live with it.* That night, I recommitted my life to Christ, and I felt so much better knowing that all my sins were washed away.

Then you pointed to me and said, "God is about to make your back as straight as an arrow." God revealed my need to you—no one else knew. When you prayed for me, you said, "Now watch her feet and ankles." Everyone could see my legs grow out as my spine was straightened. I grew three inches taller instantly. My life has not been the same since. How I praise God for His miracle-working power.

—Wanda Piston

I attended your meeting in a small town in southeast Missouri. People were talking about the miracles that were taking place in every service. I had a rather severe heart condition. The doctor said I might need surgery, and, even then, it might not help. So, I decided to come out to see if it were all true.

I had a rather severe heart condition. After you prayed for me, my neurosurgical examination showed me to have the heart of a young lady.

When I came into the auditorium, you were standing to the back of the stage area, quietly praying. You looked up when I came in, and I somehow knew you could look into the very depth of my being. Something said, "This is your night."

After your altar call, it came time to pray for the sick. I was anxious to receive, but it seemed like everyone else was getting their healing, and the service was about to end. The last person you prayed over was a teenage girl who had severe tooth misalignment. Her mother said, "She is going to have several jawbone operations that might leave her disfigured for life." Her jawbone grew back into place while we watched. Everyone was rejoicing.

Then, you looked toward me and just smiled. I let out a scream of delight. Some people laughed, but I was ready to receive. You looked at me and said, "Are you the same lady who came through the entrance, and I looked toward you? When I laid my eyes on you, God showed me your need. You have had some severe shortness of breath and some pain shooting down your left arm. It seems like you have a cement block on your chest at times." Everything you said was entirely accurate. Then, you said, "God is going to do something about it tonight." When you prayed for me, I hit the floor. When I got up, all the heaviness and difficulty breathing was gone.

The next day, my neurosurgical examination showed me to have the heart of a young lady. The doctors were completely baffled. God had worked a miracle before their eyes.

—Norma and Fred Frailey

I watched your program on TV Friday night. You said for everyone to place their hand where a healing miracle was needed. I was blind in my right eye. When you prayed, I began to see out of my right eye for the first time in twenty-six years. I now have twenty-twenty vision for the first time in my life. We are telling everyone what God can do.

(anonymous)

I am a soldier stationed in Iraq, and I am a born-again believer. We have a group of twenty-three other believers in our platoon. I received a copy of your book. I was completely engulfed in the presence of God's glory for several days. Brigade Chaplain Mark Sorenson was having services in our district. When he left, he gave us several more copies of your book. As a result, many have come to know Jesus, and we are having an outpouring among the troops here.

Chaplain Sorenson gave a copy of the book to our commanding general. We were told that he sat down and read the whole book without stopping. He has since become a believer in Christ and is seeking the baptism of the Holy Spirit. To God be all the glory.

—Tommy Sanchez

I am a United States marine currently serving in Iraq. I have always believed in God but never worshipped Him. For most of my life, I have sinned. I've done some real bad things in my life that I have regretted. My wife and I hit a hardship in our lives, and it was because of my sins. I felt lost and didn't know where to go. My wife then asked me to go to the chapel and ask God for guidance. Well, I did that to help myself and hopefully fix my life. From that point on, I found God and confessed all my sins. I opened my heart and confessed my love for Jesus.

I was feeling like a failure and thinking that Jesus had turned me away. Then I read in your book numerous times where Jesus said, "Tell them I love them." Now I know Jesus is always with me.

Well, that all sounds good, but here's where my problem set in: I led my company through the streets of Fallujah. I feel that I didn't do my job 100 percent. I took one casualty, who is in the States and doing fine. I took the least amount of casualties in any unit that went on the assault. I've beaten myself up over all my sins, and ways I could have saved that casualty differently.

Well, I went to church today, and the chaplain had your book. He said it was sent for us to learn more. I sat there feeling depressed—like I was a failure to both my family and my marines. I was thinking that Jesus had turned me away. Well, something kept telling me to grab that book on the way out. I did, and I read it nonstop. And I read numerous times Jesus saying, "Tell them I love them and look what I have already done." It has opened my eyes again. Jesus is always with me. He knows my pain. I am a sinner, but I have opened back up to Jesus. I just wanted to say thank you.

—C.

I called your prayer line number seeking someone who could pray and agree with me, as I had many needs. As we talked, you began to tell me everything about myself, including things I had forgotten. You even named my children. I had never spoken to you—and I know for sure no one had ever mentioned my name to you before. But you were told so very much. And then you said these words: "Within twenty-four hours, you will start to receive the beginnings of a complete turnaround. God has heard my prayer, and help is on the way." I was rejoicing. My wife came back the next day, and my old boss called me back to work with a large raise in pay. You were insistent that God should receive all the glory. So, I wanted to return this testimony of praise to God.

—Ernest W.
Des Moines, Iowa

I live near Sydney, Australia. I saw your television broadcast while visiting during the marketing break.

I did as you said and prayed with you for my healing. I had been struck by some type of disease. The doctors could not determine what the illness was. I lost so much weight that I was down to ninety-six pounds. I was going fast. When I touched the Tele screen, I was shocked—it felt like a current went through me. Afterward, I became very hungry. I hadn't been able to eat anything solid for about a year. Since then, all my weight has returned. I can jog for two miles. I could not do that before at all. I continue to let everyone know what God has done for me.

—Lawrence Morris

REMEMBER:

"With God all things are possible."

—Matthew 19:26

Select Scriptures

GOD RULING AND ACTING FROM HEAVEN

Acknowledge and take to heart this day that the LORD is God in heaven above and on the earth below. There is no other. Keep his decrees and commands, which I am giving you today, so that it may go well with you and your children after you and that you may live long in the land the LORD your God gives you for all time.
(Deuteronomy 4:39–40)

Look down from heaven, your holy dwelling place, and bless your people Israel and the land you have given us as you promised on oath to our forefathers, a land flowing with milk and honey.   (Deuteronomy 26:15)

I saw the LORD sitting on his throne with all the host of heaven standing around him on his right and on his left.   (1 Kings 22:19)

David praised the LORD in the presence of the whole assembly, saying, "Praise be to you, O LORD, God of our father Israel, from everlasting to everlasting. Yours, O LORD, is the greatness and the power and the glory and the majesty and the splendor, for everything in heaven and earth is yours. Yours, O LORD, is the kingdom; you are exalted as head over all. Wealth and honor come from you; you are the ruler of all things. In your hands are strength and power to exalt and give strength to all."   (1 Chronicles 29:10–12)

You alone are the LORD....*You give life to everything, and the multitudes of heaven worship you.*

(Nehemiah 9:6)

The kings of the earth take their stand and the rulers gather together against the LORD *and against his Anointed One. "Let us break their chains," they say, "and throw off their fetters." The One enthroned in heaven laughs; the Lord scoffs at them. Then he rebukes them in his anger and terrifies them in his wrath, saying, "I have installed my King on Zion, my holy hill."*

(Psalm 2:2–6)

The LORD *looks down from heaven on the sons of men to see if there are any who understand, any who seek God.*

(Psalm 14:2)

From heaven the LORD *looks down and sees all mankind; from his dwelling place he watches all who live on earth—he who forms the hearts of all, who considers everything they do. No king is saved by the size of his army; no warrior escapes by his great strength. A horse is a vain hope for deliverance; despite all its great strength it cannot save. But the eyes of the* LORD *are on those who fear him, on those whose hope is in his unfailing love, to deliver them from death and keep them alive in famine.*

(Psalm 33:13–19)

O LORD *Almighty, God of Israel, enthroned between the cherubim, you alone are God over all the kingdoms of the earth. You have made heaven and earth.*

(Isaiah 37:16)

[The Lord declares,] *"As the heavens are higher than the earth, so are my ways higher than your ways and my thoughts than your thoughts. As the rain and the snow come down from heaven, and do not return to it without watering the earth and making it bud and flourish, so that it yields seed for the sower and bread for the eater, so is my word that goes out from my mouth: It will not return to me empty, but will accomplish what I desire and achieve the purpose for which I sent it."* (Isaiah 55:9–11)

This is what the LORD says: "Heaven is my throne, and the earth is my footstool." (Isaiah 66:1)

"Bring the whole tithe into the storehouse, that there may be food in my house. Test me in this," says the LORD Almighty, "and see if I will not throw open the floodgates of heaven and pour out so much blessing that you will not have room enough for it." (Malachi 3:10)

This, then, is how you should pray: "Our Father in heaven, hallowed be your name, your kingdom come, your will be done on earth as it is in heaven." (Matthew 6:9–10)

I tell you the truth, whatever you bind on earth will be bound in heaven, and whatever you loose on earth will be loosed in heaven. Again, I tell you that if two of you on earth agree about anything you ask for, it will be done for you by my Father in heaven. (Matthew 18:18–19)

Do not call anyone on earth "father," for you have one Father, and he is in heaven.   (Matthew 23:9)

Some people brought to [Jesus] a man who was deaf and could hardly talk, and they begged him to place his hand on the man. After he took him aside, away from the crowd, Jesus put his fingers into the man's ears. Then he spit and touched the man's tongue. He looked up to heaven and with a deep sigh said to him, "Ephphatha!" (which means, "Be opened!").
(Mark 7:32–34)

I looked, and there before me was a door standing open in heaven. And the voice I had first heard speaking to me like a trumpet said, "Come up here, and I will show you what must take place after this." At once I was in the Spirit, and there before me was a throne in heaven with someone sitting on it. And the one who sat there had the appearance of jasper and car-nelian. A rainbow, resembling an emerald, encircled the throne. Surrounding the throne were twenty-four other thrones, and seated on them were twenty-four el-ders. They were dressed in white and had crowns of gold on their heads. From the throne came flashes of lightning, rumblings and peals of thunder. Before the throne, seven lamps were blazing. These are the seven spirits of God. Also before the throne there was what looked like a sea of glass, clear as crystal. In the center, around the throne, were four living creatures, and they were covered with eyes, in front and in back. The first living creature was like a lion, the second was like an ox, the third had a face like a man, the fourth was like a flying eagle. Each of the four living creatures had six wings and was covered with eyes all around, even under his wings. Day and night they never stop saying: "Holy, holy, holy is the Lord God Almighty, who was, and is, and is to come." Whenever the living creatures give glory, honor and thanks to him who sits on the throne and who lives for ever and ever, the twenty-four elders fall down before him who sits on the throne, and worship him who lives for ever and ever. They lay their crowns before the throne and say: "You are worthy, our Lord and God, to receive glory and honor and power, for you created all things, and by your will they were created and have their being."   (Revelation 4:1–11)

Then I heard every creature in heaven and on earth and under the earth and on the sea, and all that is in them, singing: "To him who sits on the throne and to the Lamb be praise and honor and glory and power, for ever and ever!"   (Revelation 5:13)

After this I looked and there before me was a great multitude that no one could count, from every nation, tribe, people and language, standing before the throne and in front of the Lamb. They were wearing white robes and were holding palm branches in their hands. And they cried out in a loud voice: "Salvation belongs to our God, who sits on the throne, and to the Lamb." All the angels were standing around the throne and around the elders and the four living creatures. They fell down on their faces before the throne and worshiped God, saying: "Amen! Praise and glory and wisdom and thanks and honor and power and strength be

to our God for ever and ever. Amen!"
                              (Revelation 7:9–12)

The seventh angel sounded his trumpet, and there were loud voices in heaven, which said: "The kingdom of the world has become the kingdom of our Lord and of his Christ, and he will reign for ever and ever." And the twenty-four elders, who were seated on their thrones before God, fell on their faces and worshiped God, saying: "We give thanks to you, Lord God Almighty, the One who is and who was, because you have taken your great power and have begun to reign. The nations were angry; and your wrath has come. The time has come for judging the dead, and for rewarding your servants the prophets and your saints and those who reverence your name, both small and great—and for destroying those who destroy the earth." Then God's temple in heaven was opened, and within his temple was seen the ark of his covenant. And there came flashes of lightning, rumblings, peals of thunder, an earthquake and a great hailstorm.
                              (Revelation 11:15–19)

Heaven Revealed on Earth/Interacting with Earth

When they reached the place God had told him about, Abraham built an altar there and arranged the wood on it. He bound his son Isaac and laid him on the altar, on top of the wood. Then he reached out his hand and took the knife to slay his son. But the angel of the LORD called out to him from heaven, "Abraham! Abraham!" "Here I am," he replied. "Do not lay a

*hand on the boy," he said. "Do not do anything to him.
Now I know that you fear God, because you have not
withheld from me your son, your only son."*

(Genesis 22:9–12)

When [Jacob] *reached a certain place, he stopped for
the night because the sun had set. Taking one of the
stones there, he put it under his head and lay down
to sleep. He had a dream in which he saw a stairway
resting on the earth, with its top reaching to heaven,
and the angels of God were ascending and descending
on it. There above it stood the LORD, and he said: "I
am the LORD, the God of your father Abraham and the
God of Isaac. I will give you and your descendants the
land on which you are lying. Your descendants will
be like the dust of the earth, and you will spread out
to the west and to the east, to the north and to the
south. All peoples on earth will be blessed through you
and your offspring. I am with you and will watch over
you wherever you go, and I will bring you back to this
land. I will not leave you until I have done what I have
promised you." When Jacob awoke from his sleep, he
thought, "Surely the LORD is in this place, and I was
not aware of it." He was afraid and said, "How awesome is this place! This is none other than the house
of God; this is the gate of heaven."*

(Genesis 28:11–17)

The angel of the LORD appeared to [Moses] *in flames
of fire from within a bush. Moses saw that though the
bush was on fire it did not burn up. So Moses thought,
"I will go over and see this strange sight—why the bush
does not burn up." When the LORD saw that he had*

gone over to look, God called to him from within the
bush, "Moses! Moses!" And Moses said, "Here I am."
"Do not come any closer," God said. "Take off your
sandals, for the place where you are standing is holy
ground."   (Exodus 3:2–5)

As [Elijah and Elisha] *were walking along and talking*
together, suddenly a chariot of fire and horses of fire ap-
peared and separated the two of them, and Elijah went
up to heaven in a whirlwind.   (2 Kings 2:11)

When Solomon finished praying, fire came down from
heaven and consumed the burnt offering and the sac-
rifices, and the glory of the LORD filled the temple. The
priests could not enter the temple of the LORD because
the glory of the LORD filled it.   (2 Chronicles 7:1–2)

The priests and the Levites stood to bless the people,
and God heard them, for their prayer reached heaven,
his holy dwelling place.   (2 Chronicles 30:27)

Stephen, full of the Holy Spirit, looked up to heaven
and saw the glory of God, and Jesus standing at the
right hand of God. "Look," he said, "I see heaven
open and the Son of Man standing at the right hand
of God."   (Acts 7:55–56)

I know a man in Christ who fourteen years ago was
caught up to the third heaven. Whether it was in the
body or out of the body I do not know—God knows.
And I know that this man—whether in the body or
apart from the body I do not know, but God knows—
was caught up to paradise. He heard inexpressible

things, things that man is not permitted to tell.
                                     (2 Corinthians 12:2–4)

ANGELS AS GOD'S HEAVENLY SERVANTS AND MESSENGERS

God sent an angel to destroy Jerusalem. But as the angel was doing so, the LORD saw it and was grieved because of the calamity and said to the angel who was destroying the people, "Enough! Withdraw your hand." The angel of the LORD was then standing at the threshing floor of Araunah the Jebusite. David looked up and saw the angel of the LORD standing between heaven and earth, with a drawn sword in his hand extended over Jerusalem. Then David and the elders, clothed in sackcloth, fell facedown....David built an altar to the LORD there and sacrificed burnt offerings and fellowship offerings. He called on the LORD, and the LORD answered him with fire from heaven on the altar of burnt offering. Then the LORD spoke to the angel, and he put his sword back into its sheath.
                                     (1 Chronicles 21:15–16, 26–27)

The LORD has established his throne in heaven, and his kingdom rules over all. Praise the LORD, you his angels, you mighty ones who do his bidding, who obey his word. Praise the LORD, all his heavenly hosts, you his servants who do his will. Praise the LORD, all his works everywhere in his dominion. Praise the LORD, O my soul.   (Psalm 103:19–22)

After the Sabbath, at dawn on the first day of the week, Mary Magdalene and the other Mary went to look at the tomb. There was a violent earthquake, for an angel of the Lord came down from heaven and, going to the tomb, rolled back the stone and sat on it. His appearance was like lightning, and his clothes were white as snow. The guards were so afraid of him that they shook and became like dead men. The angel said to the women, "Do not be afraid, for I know that you are looking for Jesus, who was crucified. He is not here; he has risen, just as he said."

(Matthew 28:1–6)

And there were shepherds living out in the fields nearby, keeping watch over their flocks at night. An angel of the Lord appeared to them, and the glory of the Lord shone around them, and they were terrified. But the angel said to them, "Do not be afraid. I bring you good news of great joy that will be for all the people. Today in the town of David a Savior has been born to you; he is Christ the Lord. This will be a sign to you: You will find a baby wrapped in cloths and lying in a manger." Suddenly a great company of the heavenly host appeared with the angel, praising God and saying, "Glory to God in the highest, and on earth peace to men on whom his favor rests." When the angels had left them and gone into heaven, the shepherds said to one another, "Let's go to Bethlehem and see this thing that has happened, which the Lord has told us about." (Luke 2:8–15)

[Jesus] *withdrew about a stone's throw beyond them, knelt down and prayed, "Father, if you are willing, take this cup from me; yet not my will, but yours be done." An angel from heaven appeared to him and strengthened him.* (Luke 22:41–43)

*Are not all angels ministering spirits sent to serve those
who will inherit salvation?*   (Hebrews 1:14)

Jesus' Heavenly Origins/Mission from Heaven

*An angel of the Lord appeared to [Joseph] in a dream
and said, "Joseph son of David, do not be afraid to take
Mary home as your wife, because what is conceived in
her is from the Holy Spirit. She will give birth to a son,
and you are to give him the name Jesus, because he
will save his people from their sins." All this took place
to fulfill what the Lord had said through the prophet:
"The virgin will be with child and will give birth to a
son, and they will call him Immanuel"—which means,
"God with us."*   (Matthew 1:20–23)

*As soon as Jesus was baptized, he went up out of the
water. At that moment heaven was opened, and he saw
the Spirit of God descending like a dove and lighting
on him. And a voice from heaven said, "This is my
Son, whom I love; with him I am well pleased."*
(Matthew 3:16–17)

*John gave this testimony: "I saw the Spirit come down
from heaven as a dove and remain on him."*
                                        (John 1:32)

*I tell you the truth, you shall see heaven open, and the
angels of God ascending and descending on the Son of
Man.*   (John 1:51)

*"It is my Father who gives you the true bread from
heaven. For the bread of God is he who comes down*

from heaven and gives life to the world."...Then Jesus declared, "I am the bread of life." (John 6:32–33, 35)

I have come down from heaven not to do my will but to do the will of him who sent me. And this is the will of him who sent me, that I shall lose none of all that he has given me, but raise them up at the last day. For my Father's will is that everyone who looks to the Son and believes in him shall have eternal life, and I will raise him up at the last day. (John 6:38–40)

[Jesus said,] *"Now my heart is troubled, and what shall I say? 'Father, save me from this hour'? No, it was for this very reason I came to this hour. Father, glorify your name!" Then a voice came from heaven, "I have glorified it, and will glorify it again."*
(John 12:27–28)

The Nature of Heaven/God's Kingdom

I am always with you [God]; you hold me by my right hand. You guide me with your counsel, and afterward you will take me into glory. Whom have I in heaven but you? And earth has nothing I desire besides you. My flesh and my heart may fail, but God is the strength of my heart and my portion forever. (Psalm 73:23–26)

I will declare that your love stands firm forever, that you established your faithfulness in heaven itself.
(Psalm 89:2)

Anyone who breaks one of the least of these command-ments and teaches others to do the same will be called least in the kingdom of heaven, but whoever practices and teaches these commands will be called great in the kingdom of heaven. (Matthew 5:19)

Not everyone who says to me, "Lord, Lord," will enter the kingdom of heaven, but only he who does the will of my Father who is in heaven...For whoever does the will of my Father in heaven is my brother and sister and mother. (Matthew 7:21; 12:50)

Unless you change and become like little children, you will never enter the kingdom of heaven. Therefore, whoever humbles himself like this child is the greatest in the kingdom of heaven....See that you do not look down on one of these little ones. For I tell you that their angels in heaven always see the face of my Father in heaven. (Matthew 18:3–4, 10)

Jesus said, "Let the little children come to me, and do not hinder them, for the kingdom of heaven belongs to such as these." (Matthew 19:14)

At the resurrection people will neither marry nor be given in marriage; they will be like the angels in heaven. (Matthew 22:30)

But love your enemies, do good to them, and lend to them without expecting to get anything back. Then your reward will be great, and you will be sons of the Most High, because he is kind to the ungrateful and wicked. Be merciful, just as your Father is merciful. (Luke 6:35–36)

There will be more rejoicing in heaven over one sinner who repents than over ninety-nine righteous persons who do not need to repent. (Luke 15:7)

For the kingdom of God is not a matter of eating and drinking, but of righteousness, peace and joy in the Holy Spirit.   (Romans 14:17)

The acts of the sinful nature are obvious: sexual immorality, impurity and debauchery; idolatry and witchcraft; hatred, discord, jealousy, fits of rage, selfish ambition, dissensions, factions and envy; drunkenness, orgies, and the like. I warn you, as I did before, that those who live like this will not inherit the kingdom of God. But the fruit of the Spirit is love, joy, peace, patience, kindness, goodness, faithfulness, gentleness and self-control. Against such things there is no law.
(Galatians 5:19–23)

Since we are surrounded by such a great cloud of witnesses, let us throw off everything that hinders and the sin that so easily entangles, and let us run with perseverance the race marked out for us.
(Hebrews 12:1)

The wisdom that comes from heaven is first of all pure; then peace-loving, considerate, submissive, full of mercy and good fruit, impartial and sincere.
(James 3:17)

In keeping with his promise we are looking forward to a new heaven and a new earth, the home of righteousness.   (2 Peter 3:13)

JESUS CHRIST RULING FROM HEAVEN

Then Jesus came to them and said, "All authority in heaven and on earth has been given to me. Therefore go and make disciples of all nations, baptizing them in the name of the Father and of the Son and of the Holy Spirit, and teaching them to obey everything I have commanded you. And surely I am with you always, to the very end of the age."

(Matthew 28:18–20)

[Jesus] *said to them, "Go into all the world and preach the good news to all creation. Whoever believes and is baptized will be saved, but whoever does not believe will be condemned. And these signs will accompany those who believe: In my name they will drive out demons; they will speak in new tongues; they will pick up snakes with their hands; and when they drink deadly poison, it will not hurt them at all; they will place their hands on sick people, and they will get well." After the Lord Jesus had spoken to them, he was taken up into heaven and he sat at the right hand of God.*

(Mark 16:15–19)

[Jesus said,] *"I am going to send you what my Father has promised; but stay in the city until you have been clothed with power from on high." When he had led them out to the vicinity of Bethany, he lifted up his hands and blessed them. While he was blessing them, he left them and was taken up into heaven.*

(Luke 24:49–51)

[God] *hath raised us up together, and made us sit together in heavenly places in Christ Jesus.*

(Ephesians 2:6 KJV)

[Jesus] *is the image of the invisible God, the firstborn over all creation. For by him all things were created: things in heaven and on earth, visible and invisible,*

whether thrones or powers or rulers or authorities; all things were created by him and for him. He is before all things, and in him all things hold together.
                                        (Colossians 1:15–17)

The Son is the radiance of God's glory and the exact representation of his being, sustaining all things by his powerful word. After he had provided purification for sins, he sat down at the right hand of the Majesty in heaven. So he became as much superior to the angels as the name he has inherited is superior to theirs.   (Hebrews 1:3–4)

We do have such a high priest, who sat down at the right hand of the throne of the Majesty in heaven, and who serves in the sanctuary, the true tabernacle set up by the Lord, not by man....Christ did not enter a manmade sanctuary that was only a copy of the true one; he entered heaven itself, now to appear for us in God's presence.   (Hebrews 8:1–2; 9:24)

Jesus Christ...has gone into heaven and is at God's right hand—with angels, authorities and powers in submission to him.   (1 Peter 3:21–22)

HEAVENLY BOOKS OF RECORD/BOOK OF LIFE/ NAMES WRITTEN IN HEAVEN

Your eyes saw my unformed body. All the days ordained for me were written in your book before one of them came to be.   (Psalm 139:16)

I have given you authority to trample on snakes and scorpions and to overcome all the power of the enemy;

nothing will harm you. However, do not rejoice that the spirits submit to you, but rejoice that your names are written in heaven.   (Luke 10:19–20)

I ask you, loyal yokefellow, help these women who have contended at my side in the cause of the gospel, along with Clement and the rest of my fellow workers, whose names are in the book of life.   (Philippians 4:3)

You have come to Mount Zion, to the heavenly Jerusalem, the city of the living God. You have come to thousands upon thousands of angels in joyful assembly, to the church of the firstborn, whose names are written in heaven. You have come to God, the judge of all men, to the spirits of righteous men made perfect, to Jesus the mediator of a new covenant, and to the sprinkled blood that speaks a better word than the blood of Abel.   (Hebrews 12:22–24)

He who overcomes will, like them, be dressed in white. I will never blot out his name from the book of life, but will acknowledge his name before my Father and his angels.   (Revelation 3:5)

And I saw the dead, great and small, standing before the throne, and books were opened. Another book was opened, which is the book of life. The dead were judged according to what they had done as recorded in the books. The sea gave up the dead that were in it, and death and Hades gave up the dead that were in them, and each person was judged according to what he had done. Then death and Hades were thrown into the lake of fire. The lake of fire is the second death. If

anyone's name was not found written in the book of life, he was thrown into the lake of fire.
                                        (Revelation 20:12–15)

Nothing impure will ever enter [the Holy City], nor will anyone who does what is shameful or deceitful, but only those whose names are written in the Lamb's book of life.   (Revelation 21:27)

HEAVENLY/ETERNAL REWARDS

Blessed are those who are persecuted because of righteousness, for theirs is the kingdom of heaven. Blessed are you when people insult you, persecute you and falsely say all kinds of evil against you because of me. Rejoice and be glad, because great is your reward in heaven, for in the same way they persecuted the prophets who were before you.   (Matthew 5:10–12)

Love your enemies and pray for those who persecute you, that you may be sons of your Father in heaven. He causes his sun to rise on the evil and the good, and sends rain on the righteous and the unrighteous. If you love those who love you, what reward will you get? Are not even the tax collectors doing that? And if you greet only your brothers, what are you doing more than others? Do not even pagans do that? Be perfect, therefore, as your heavenly Father is perfect. Be careful not to do your "acts of righteousness" before men, to be seen by them. If you do, you will have no reward from your Father in heaven. So when you give to the needy, do not announce it with trumpets, as the hypocrites do in the synagogues and on the streets, to be honored by men. I tell you the truth, they have received their reward in full. But when you give to the needy, do not let your left hand know what your right hand is doing, so that your giving may be in secret. Then your Father, who sees what is done in secret, will reward you. And when you pray, do not be like the hypocrites, for they love to pray standing in the synagogues and on the street corners to be seen by men. I tell you the truth, they have received their reward in full. But when you pray, go into your room, close the door and pray to your Father, who is unseen. Then your Father, who sees what is done in secret, will reward you.

(Matthew 5:44–6:6)

Do not store up for yourselves treasures on earth, where moth and rust destroy, and where thieves break in and steal. Store up for yourselves treasures in heaven, where moth and rust do not destroy, and where thieves do not break in and steal. (Matthew 6:19–20)

Whoever acknowledges me before men, I will also acknowledge him before my Father in heaven. But whoever disowns me before men, I will disown him before my Father in heaven. (Matthew 10:32–33)

Anyone who receives a prophet because he is a prophet will receive a prophet's reward, and anyone who receives a righteous man because he is a righteous man will receive a righteous man's reward. And if anyone gives even a cup of cold water to one of these little ones because he is my disciple, I tell you the truth, he will certainly not lose his reward. (Matthew 10:41–42)

The kingdom of heaven is like treasure hidden in a field. When a man found it, he hid it again, and then in his joy went and sold all he had and bought that field. Again, the kingdom of heaven is like a merchant looking for fine pearls. When he found one of great value, he went away and sold everything he had and bought it. (Matthew 13:44–46)

The Son of Man is going to come in his Father's glory with his angels, and then he will reward each person according to what he has done. (Matthew 16:27)

Blessed are you when men hate you, when they exclude you and insult you and reject your name as evil, because of the Son of Man. Rejoice in that day and leap for joy, because great is your reward in heaven. For that is how their fathers treated the prophets. (Luke 6:22–23)

Do not be afraid, little flock, for your Father has been pleased to give you the kingdom. Sell your possessions and give to the poor. Provide purses for yourselves that will not wear out, a treasure in heaven that will not be exhausted, where no thief comes near and no moth destroys. For where your treasure is, there your heart will be also. (Luke 12:32–34)

So neither he who plants nor he who waters is anything, but only God, who makes things grow. The man who plants and the man who waters have one purpose, and each will be rewarded according to his own labor. For we are God's fellow workers; you are God's field, God's building. By the grace God has given me, I laid a foundation as an expert builder, and someone else is building on it. But each one should be careful how he builds. For no one can lay any foundation other than the one already laid, which is Jesus Christ. If any man builds on this foundation using gold, silver, costly stones, wood, hay or straw, his work will be shown for what it is, because the Day will bring it to light. It will be revealed with fire, and the fire will test the quality of each man's work. If what he has built survives, he will receive his reward. If it is burned up, he will suffer loss; he himself will be saved, but only as one escaping through the flames.

(1 Corinthians 3:7–15)

For we must all appear before the judgment seat of Christ, that each one may receive what is due him for the things done while in the body, whether good or bad. (2 Corinthians 5:10)

Serve wholeheartedly, as if you were serving the Lord, not men, because you know that the Lord will reward everyone for whatever good he does, whether he is slave or free. (Ephesians 6:7–8)

Whatever you do, work at it with all your heart, as working for the Lord, not for men, since you know that you will receive an inheritance from the Lord as a reward. It is the Lord Christ you are serving.

(Colossians 3:23–24)

Do not throw away your confidence; it will be richly rewarded. You need to persevere so that when you have done the will of God, you will receive what he has promised. For in just a very little while, "He who is coming will come and will not delay. But my righteous one will live by faith. And if he shrinks back, I will not be pleased with him." But we are not of those who shrink back and are destroyed, but of those who believe and are saved.   (Hebrews 10:35–39)

By faith Moses, when he had grown up, refused to be known as the son of Pharaoh's daughter. He chose to be mistreated along with the people of God rather than to enjoy the pleasures of sin for a short time. He regarded disgrace for the sake of Christ as of greater value than the treasures of Egypt, because he was looking ahead to his reward.   (Hebrews 11:24–26)

Watch out that you do not lose what you have worked for, but that you may be rewarded fully. Anyone who runs ahead and does not continue in the teaching of Christ does not have God; whoever continues in the teaching has both the Father and the Son.

(2 John 1:8–9)

Him who overcomes I will make a pillar in the temple of my God. Never again will he leave it. I will write on him the name of my God and the name of the city of my God, the new Jerusalem, which is coming down out of heaven from my God; and I will also write on him my new name.   (Revelation 3:12)

Behold, I am coming soon! My reward is with me, and I will give to everyone according to what he has done. I am the Alpha and the Omega, the First and the Last, the Beginning and the End. Blessed are those who wash their robes, that they may have the right to the tree of life and may go through the gates into the city.

Outside are the dogs, those who practice magic arts, the sexually immoral, the murderers, the idolaters and everyone who loves and practices falsehood. I, Jesus, have sent my angel to give you this testimony for the churches. I am the Root and the Offspring of David, and the bright Morning Star.

(Revelation 22:12–16)

JESUS CHRIST'S RETURN FROM HEAVEN/RULE OVER EARTH

In my vision at night I looked, and there before me was one like a son of man, coming with the clouds of heaven. He approached the Ancient of Days and was led into his presence. He was given authority, glory and sovereign power; all peoples, nations and men of every language worshiped him. His dominion is an everlasting dominion that will not pass away, and his kingdom is one that will never be destroyed.

(Daniel 7:13–14)

In the future you will see the Son of Man sitting at the right hand of the Mighty One and coming on the clouds of heaven.   (Matthew 26:64)

[Jesus] said to them: "It is not for you to know the times or dates the Father has set by his own authority. But you will receive power when the Holy Spirit comes on you; and you will be my witnesses in Jerusalem, and in all Judea and Samaria, and to the ends of the earth." After he said this, he was taken up before their very eyes, and a cloud hid him from their sight. They were looking intently up into the sky as he was going, when

suddenly two men dressed in white stood beside them. "Men of Galilee," they said, "why do you stand here looking into the sky? This same Jesus, who has been taken from you into heaven, will come back in the same way you have seen him go into heaven."
(Acts 1:7–11)

[God] made known to us the mystery of his will according to his good pleasure, which he purposed in Christ, to be put into effect when the times will have reached their fulfillment—to bring all things in heaven and on earth together under one head, even Christ.
(Ephesians 1:9–10)

God exalted [Jesus] to the highest place and gave him the name that is above every name, that at the name of Jesus every knee should bow, in heaven and on earth and under the earth, and every tongue confess that Jesus Christ is Lord, to the glory of God the Father.
(Philippians 2:9–11)

Our citizenship is in heaven. And we eagerly await a Savior from there, the Lord Jesus Christ, who, by the power that enables him to bring everything under his control, will transform our lowly bodies so that they will be like his glorious body.   (Philippians 3:20–21)

Since, then, you have been raised with Christ, set your hearts on things above, where Christ is seated at the right hand of God. Set your minds on things above, not on earthly things. For you died, and your life is now hidden with Christ in God. When Christ, who is your life, appears, then you also will appear with him in glory.
(Colossians 3:1–4)

The Lord Jesus [will be] *revealed from heaven in blazing fire with his powerful angels. He will punish those who do not know God...on the day he comes to be glorified in his holy people and to be marveled at among all those who have believed.*

(2 Thessalonians 1:7–8, 10)

I looked, and there before me was a white horse! Its rider held a bow, and he was given a crown, and he rode out as a conqueror bent on conquest.

(Revelation 6:2)

I saw heaven standing open and there before me was a white horse, whose rider is called Faithful and True. With justice he judges and makes war. His eyes are like blazing fire, and on his head are many crowns. He has a name written on him that no one knows but he himself. He is dressed in a robe dipped in blood, and his name is the Word of God. The armies of heaven were following him, riding on white horses and dressed in fine linen, white and clean. Out of his mouth comes a sharp sword with which to strike down the nations. "He will rule them with an iron scepter." He treads the winepress of the fury of the wrath of God Almighty. On his robe and on his thigh he has this name written: King of Kings and Lord of Lords. (Revelation 19:11–16)

Our Heavenly Home/Eternal Life

In my Father's house are many rooms; if it were not so, I would have told you. I am going there to prepare a place for you. And if I go and prepare a place for you, I will come back and take you to be with me that you also may be where I am.   (John 14:2–3)

Therefore we do not lose heart. Though outwardly we are wasting away, yet inwardly we are being renewed day by day. For our light and momentary troubles are achieving for us an eternal glory that far outweighs them all. So we fix our eyes not on what is seen, but on what is unseen. For what is seen is temporary, but what is unseen is eternal. Now we know that if the earthly tent we live in is destroyed, we have a building from God, an eternal house in heaven, not built by human hands. Meanwhile we groan, longing to be clothed with our heavenly dwelling, because when we are clothed, we will not be found naked. For while we are in this tent, we groan and are burdened, because we do not wish to be unclothed but to be clothed with our heavenly dwelling, so that what is mortal may be swallowed up by life. Now it is God who has made us for this very purpose and has given us the Spirit as a deposit, guaranteeing what is to come. Therefore we are always confident and know that as long as we are at home in the body we are away from the Lord. We live by faith, not by sight. We are confident, I say, and would prefer to be away from the body and at home with the Lord. So we make it our goal to please him, whether we are at home in the body or away from it.
                (2 Corinthians 4:16–5:9)

We have heard of your faith in Christ Jesus and of the love you have for all the saints—the faith and love that spring from the hope that is stored up for you in heaven and that you have already heard about in the word of truth, the gospel that has come to you.

(Colossians 1:4–6)

Brothers, we do not want you to be ignorant about those who fall asleep, or to grieve like the rest of men, who have no hope. We believe that Jesus died and rose again and so we believe that God will bring with Jesus those who have fallen asleep in him. According to the Lord's own word, we tell you that we who are still alive, who are left till the coming of the Lord, will certainly not precede those who have fallen asleep. For the Lord himself will come down from heaven, with a loud command, with the voice of the archangel and with the trumpet call of God, and the dead in Christ will rise first. After that, we who are still alive and are left will be caught up together with them in the clouds to meet the Lord in the air. And so we will be with the Lord forever.   (1 Thessalonians 4:13–17)

Praise be to the God and Father of our Lord Jesus Christ! In his great mercy he has given us new birth into a living hope through the resurrection of Jesus Christ from the dead, and into an inheritance that can never perish, spoil or fade—kept in heaven for you, who through faith are shielded by God's power until the coming of the salvation that is ready to be revealed in the last time.   (1 Peter 1:3–5)

I saw the Holy City, the new Jerusalem, coming down out of heaven from God, prepared as a bride beautifully dressed for her husband. And I heard a loud voice from the throne saying, "Now the dwelling of God is with men, and he will live with them. They will be his people, and God himself will be with them and be their God. He will wipe every tear from their eyes. There will be no more death or mourning or crying or pain, for the old order of things has passed away." He who was seated on the throne said, "I am making everything new!" (Revelation 21:2–5)

And the city had no need of the sun, neither of the moon, to shine in it: for the glory of God did lighten it, and the Lamb is the light thereof.

(Revelation 21:23 KJV)

Index

About the Author

Richard Sigmund (1941–2010) was born in Des Moines, Iowa. His grandfather was praying as Richard was being born, and the Lord told him, "Through him, I will answer prayer." Whose prayer? The prayer of his great-grandfather, who was a Spirit-filled, Jewish, circuit-riding preacher during the Civil War.

The Lord first appeared to Richard when he was four years old. As a child, he started preaching in a country Methodist church in Iowa. His grandfather knew healing evangelist Jack Coe Sr., and Rev. Coe brought Richard to Omaha in 1949 to preach. While the boy who became known as "Little Richard" preached, the anointing came upon him, and he saw angels.

When he was about nine years old, he presented the gospel before the meetings of world-renowned evangelist and miracle worker A. A. Allen. Richard was with Allen for about ten years; tutors enabled him to maintain his schoolwork while he was on the road. Also during that time, Richard was with evangelist Lee Girard and presented his testimony during William Branham meetings.

In his early twenties, Richard had a fruitful ministry for a time in Phoenix, Arizona, and then held tent meetings with considerable success among the Navajo in northern Arizona and in other revival meetings around the country. In 1974, while he was ministering at a small church in Bartlesville, Oklahoma, he was declared dead for eight hours after a traffic accident, during which he had his experiences of heaven and hell.

Over the years, Richard preached the gospel through television programs, radio broadcasts, and speaking engagements. He was in meetings with Kathryn Kuhlman and Oral Roberts, and he was interviewed by Pat Robertson. Richard ministered in England, Scotland, Australia, South Africa, Kenya, and many other countries. In South Africa, he followed David Nunn and Morris Cerullo in a special series of meetings. It was Rex Humbard who encouraged him to tell his story of a place called heaven.

In the early 1990s, Richard met his wife, Priscilla, a fellow native of Iowa. After living in Texas and Missouri, they returned to Iowa, where they based their organization, Cleft of the Rock Ministries.